Slim and Spicy

By Manjit Kaur Ruprai

ISBN-13:9780995459915

Published by Ann Jaloba Publishing, 26 Tapton Mount Close, Sheffield S10 5DJ

the moral right of Manjit Kaur Ruprai to be identified as the author has been asserted in accordance with the copyright design and patents act 1988

Note to Readers

DEDICATION

In memory of my late father Kuldip Singh Ruprai

A special thank you to my sister Teerth and Mum Balvinder who have been there for me.

A huge thank you to Robin and Jayne, who have continued to support me and put up with me.

A massive thank you to my cheeky nephews Amar and Jay and my beautiful niece Roop for making me smile every day.

A big thank you to Afsha Malik, India Kang, Sarah Crossland, Shobana Patel and Jevanjot Kaur Sihra for taking the time out to contribute to this book. And an extra special thank you to Steve Miller and Ann Jaloba for mentoring and coaching me. Couldn't have done what I do without you.

Slim and Spicy

Foreword

By Vishal Morjaria

I was so pleased to be asked to write a foreword for this book. I know from my own work as a mindset coach how important health, fitness and appearance can be in making people truly happy.

Manjit and I live in the same city and are both examples of how health and wellbeing are beginning to take a much more important role in the story of our communities. We have both been moved and inspired by many of the same strengths and possibilities we see in the communities around us. It's great to be able to welcome a book into print which reflects this change.

Manjit shows how it is possible to keep the wonderful life enhancing traditions of eating to celebrate and enjoying being with family and friends while making the lifestyle healthier. Manjit's attitude, positivity and can do attitude shines through every sentence of this book. She knows from her own experience how unhealthy patterns of eating in the Asian community can be. She is in the forefront of the growing movement to change this.

With her Asian Exclusive Weight Loss Programme she has already given a huge boost to the cause of helping us become healthier and happier and this book is going to get her message across to a much wider audience.

For a short book it covers an amazing amount, from making healthy curries to how to be a glowing bride. Her case studies are inspiring and if you want to know how to change your mindset and empower yourself, her hypnotherapy techniques will get you on the right path. Just read on and you will see what I mean.

Vishal Morjaria
Award winning Author

My story: why I wrote this book

Losing my father at a very young age to heart disease and

realising that I could go the same way was my wake-up call.

As I found out more and more about diet and lifestyle, I

realised how dangerous the traditional Asian diet and lifestyle

could be. And I began my mission to change it.

I had a 15-year-long career in mental health services and education before I decided to follow my instincts to train as a clinical hypnotherapist as I have always had a keen interest in working with people. After years of working in various areas of hypnotherapy I found the areas of weight loss of particular interest as I gained weight many years ago, so I continued my professional development and took a master class in weight loss with Steve Miller from the popular TV series *Fat Families*. I have also contributed a chapter on Weightloss in the Asian Community to the book *The Hypnotherapy Experts* by Ann Jaloba.

My family tragedies could have been avoided
Having high blood pressure, diabetes, heart disease and premature death in my family due to unhealthy eating, weight loss continues to be my area of particular interest and expertise.

My grandmother died of ischemic heart disease at the age of 60 and my grandfather died of a heart attack at the age of 65.

My father also had a heart attack at the age of 47, but luckily he survived and went through triple bypass surgery. But after going for another operation he suffered the same fate as my grandma and died of ischemic heart disease at the age of 51. In this day and age this was so young to die.

"I look fat"

Having these problems in my family and being a self-confessed secret eater, I had to alter my eating habits. This came home to me hard when a friend told me I looked fat.

I didn't want the same things to happen to me as to my family, so this was my wake-up call. It made me take a major reality check of my eating habits. No one had ever said I looked 'fat' before. I felt embarrassed each time I looked in the mirror or at my photos as I realised this was what everyone else saw. That one word 'fat' made me want my old body back and motivated and drove me to do something about my weight. If my friend had not been direct and honest and had not told me I looked 'fat' I am sure I would have carried on and would have become even bigger.

Looking back at my eating habits, I have realised that it is all too easy to put the weight on and it takes a lot of hard work and effort to take it off and to keep it off long term. Although my friend's words seemed offensive to me at the time, I now thank him for saying I looked 'fat'. That one word led me to shift the weight and eventually I had the inspiration to work with other people with weight issues. If I was fat now, I am sure no one would want to work with me as a weight loss coach and hypnotherapist. I would be a hypocrite for telling others to slim down if I cannot do it myself.

A lot of people that I meet are unaware that I was once fat. When I carry out a workshop, I will usually show the attendees my fat photo and they are surprised that I looked like that. Sharing my story usually builds that connection as I am not just some slim hypnotherapist preaching to other individuals how they can be slim. Clients usually feel a connection and my fat story resonates with them.

I had always been slim and petite at 4ft 10in, but I put on about two stones after the loss of my father. I started eating cakes and other junk food nearly every day and before I knew it the weight crept on.

I think I lost the sense of caring in the world after losing my father at such a young age so I caused destruction to my own body. Emotional eating is a common problem and I see it all the time in my practice. People eat when they are happy, excited, stressed, sad or even when under pressure. For some individuals, emotions dictate how they eat. How many times have you heard the phrase: 'I feel stressed out. I need chocolate.'

Emotions are always there
Eating for comfort or to satisfy emotions turns into a vicious cycle that many are unable to get out of as emotions are always there. We all experience various emotions every day whether they are happy or sad. This is natural for all human beings, but where it goes wrong is if people allow their emotions to dictate how they eat. Unfortunately, eating for comfort does not fix your emotional problems or state. You end up feeling worse than you did as you *will* put weight on.

That is just what happened to me. So not only do you suffer emotionally you also cause destruction to your body. Piling on the weight then leads to chronic illnesses. Unless you find a way to control your eating, you will go through this vicious cycle throughout your whole life.

I have realised that weight is all too easy to put on, but it takes a lot of hard work and dedication to burn it off and most importantly to keep it off.

When I became overweight I had to work really hard to burn off the fat. I had a strict exercise regime where I attended a gym at least four times a week. I did cardio for at least 45 minutes to an hour each time, which would work up a sweat and then I would go on the toning tables to relax and would do some weights.

Still enjoying food

To achieve effective weight loss I have had to gain a real understanding of having to balance my eating while at the same time enjoying my food with a little treat here and there. It is impossible to maintain a rigid diet of juices, salads and some of the other common diets that you hear about in the media.

We are all human and can only carry on for so long being deprived of the foods that we crave for and enjoy.

I have tried a rigid diet of juices, salads and soups and I would be starving by the end of the day leading me to eat more and binge to satisfy those cravings. I craved real food. I couldn't maintain these diets so within a few days I would give up. I now eat healthily about 80 percent of the time and enjoy a little treat here and there about 20 percent of the time and I have continued to carry on exercising. This has helped me to maintain a healthy balance and consequently a stable weight many years on.

Each time I felt like giving up and wanted to binge on rubbish I could hear my friend's words in my head saying 'you look fat' and that made me carry on and never give up. This is why a lot of my weight loss programmes are direct and authoritarian, but yet positive and supportive.

I do not believe the fluffy approach works with clients. I

learned this from my friend who was direct with me and that led me to take action.

Taking responsibility

I recently visited my GP who tested my blood pressure, glucose and cholesterol. Although everything else was normal my GP mentioned my cholesterol is slightly high at 5.40 and that I need to keep an eye on it. My jaw dropped open when he told me as I do cardio at least three times a week and take a brisk walk for at least 45 minutes a day. I also watch what I eat, most mornings eating porridge for breakfast, sandwich for lunch with carrot sticks and a healthy Indian meal at night. I treat myself about three times a week with something that I fancy like, a slice of cake, a small piece of chocolate, or crisps. I very rarely eat takeaways. With my active healthy, lifestyle I asked my GP how my cholesterol can be slightly high? He mentioned that I could have hereditary cholesterol from my family. I know that I have a family history of high cholesterol from eating unhealthy Indian food. According to Heart UK, one in every 500 individuals is affected with hereditary cholesterol.

I am now even stricter with what I eat and have restricted my treats even further as I do not want heart disease and clogged up arteries. Each time I fancy something fattening and unhealthy I just think of becoming fat again and the cholesterol seeping through my arteries. Six months on my cholesterol is back to normal at 4.3 as I made some further lifestyle changes and altered my eating completely. You can change your lifestyle too if you want it bad enough.

If your GP has told you that you need to lose weight for health reasons this should be enough incentive to do something about it. The good news is that hypnotherapy can help to give you back control over food, as I will show you throughout this book.

A tip that you might want to use as this works for me when I get the munchies:

1. Place a block of butter in your hands and close your eyes.
2. Think today is the day you will let go of all the excess fat and become lighter. If you carry on the way you are you will remain that fat arse.
3. Just imagine the butter seeping through your arteries
4. Now just imagine you looking amazing as all that butter melts away.

I work with a diverse clientele on my *6-Week Straight Talking Motivational Weight Loss Programme.* However, I am really passionate about weight loss for the Asian community. This led me to develop an *Asian Exclusive Weight Loss Programme* and to write this book so that I can share my experiences and educate others. My message is that you do not have to be on a rigid diet to experience weight loss and that Asian food does not have to be unhealthy. *The Asian Exclusive Weight Loss Programme* is tailored for the Asian community and it can be delivered in Punjabi, Hindi or Urdu as well as English. Individuals do not necessarily have to have hypnosis, but I will use my strong coaching style to help and support individuals to get into shape and regain healthiness.

I hope you enjoy this book and get an insight into the changes which can be made to enjoy a healthy Asian lifestyle and diet.

To a Healthy Future

Manjit

CONTENTS

Slim and Spicy

Chapter One

Health, diet and beliefs in the Asian community

I am on a mission to change the culture I grew up in and make it healthier. I know I'm working with a trend. Modern Asians are going to leave behind all the old habits which did our parents' generation so much harm.

Chronic health issues such as heart disease and diabetes are more common in the UK's Asian communities than in other ethnic groups. Experts are unsure why this is the case, but there are strong links related to unhealthy eating, doing too little exercise and then gaining excess weight.

NHS statistics show that Asians are six times more likely to have diabetes than the general population and the risk of dying early from coronary heart disease is twice as high compared to the overall population. Diabetes also leads to other health issues such as glaucoma, blindness, kidney disease and dental problems to name just a few. Heart disease covers a whole range of serious health problems such as stroke, ischemic heart disease, and heart attack; all of which can lead to early death.

While life expectancy in general is increasing, Asian men are lagging badly behind. The average life expectancy for a white male in the UK is now 81 years, but is just 65 years for Asian males. These figures are shocking.

This is not just a British problem. Research carried out in the USA by the Agency for Healthcare Research and Quality (AHRQ) has found some interesting links as to why the Asian community there suffer more diabetes and heart disease than any other group. The results are fascinating, some of the things it found I can relate to amongst my own family and friends. The research shows that there are six main areas where Asians face a number of barriers compared to other groups in making lifestyle changes which would reduce the risk of cardiovascular disease. These are:

- gender roles
- body image
- physical activity
- cultural priorities
- cultural identity
- explanatory model of disease (Asians believe that having an illness is not in their control).

Beliefs about butter and ghee

The research shows that in Asian households women are generally responsible for food preparation and raising the children. If, in an extended family the eldest female or male has an influence over the dietary decisions there can be a resistance to making dietary modifications such as a reduction in consuming butter and ghee. Butter and ghee carry strong messages in Asian food culture, they are seen as representing nurturing (especially when they are featuring in meals served at social gatherings). So, In the Asian community there is a reluctance to reduce their use.

I have seen this myself, in my local Sikh temple one lady said to me that she is seen as tight-fisted as she does not cook with butter and ghee, (instead she cooks her curries in oil as it is much healthier). This is just one small example of a strong tendency to reject the belief that consuming less butter and ghee will improve health. Many people are still oblivious to the health problems a high-fat diet can cause. My own family history is very sad in this regard. My mother has many health problems and my father died an early death.

Yet, my mother still believes that ghee and butter are not harmful. She will often say that ghee is good for the joints and that it keeps them flexible with all the grease. It's a strange model of the human body – believing that you can apply ghee to creaking knee and hip joints in the same way as you might apply WD40 to a creaking door! My mother gets this belief from her roots back

Fat to Fit as Bollywood gets the health message

"Fat and Fit, both words are related directly to an individual's health. Nowadays, everyone wants to be fit and fine irrespective of one's field. A fit body is the most important when it comes to entertainment world," says blogger Sumit Chopra. See the before and after shots at http://www.findhealthtips.com/fat-to-fit-bollywood-actresses/

in India and she is very resistant to change. She also suffers with high blood pressure (reaching over 200 at one point), but yet she still chooses to sprinkle extra salt on her vegetables and salad.

It affects my wider family as well. My aunt is under the impression that she cooks healthily and will often ask me for tips about healthy cooking, as she knows I am a weight loss expert. I have educated her on the harmful effects of ghee and butter, but I have seen her time and time again cooking in ghee and using excessive amounts of butter.

It is no wonder that most of her family are overweight and have health issues such as diabetes, and this is before they reach the age of 40.

Belief about taking time for yourself
Beliefs about exercise are also stopping people developing a healthy lifestyle. In certain Asian communities taking time out to exercise is seen as taking time out from the family and it is therefore deemed as inappropriate.

It means a lot of Asian women find it difficult to exercise as there is an expectation that they should stay at home and tend to the family's needs, rather than taking time out for themselves.

Exercise has long been undervalued and under-emphasised, and this belief goes back for generations.

There is a lack of understanding of what happens to the human body during exercise. For example, an increased heart rate during exercise is seen as a cause for alarm rather than what would be expected to happen.

Then there are societal pressures. There is a strong cultural belief, for both men and women, that time outside of work should be spent helping or caring for relatives and children and not spent on leisure activities such as exercising.

Body image: is larger good?
Then there is the issue of body image. Traditionally, there is a belief

that being a larger size also indicates good health. This is something that I have experienced as my mother and other family members will sometimes refer to larger women as being healthy and the slimmer women as being unwell and scrawny-looking.

I was bigger years ago, but when I see family members now they remark on my body shape. They say they preferred me before, when I was carrying lots of excess weight to my current slim and healthy body shape.

They often tell me that I look weak and unhealthy and they will always ask if my health is okay. These beliefs are a reflection of the

All change

I am pleased to see this change reflected in the attitude of some of my clients. 27 year old Rabinder, believes that Indian food has become healthier in today's generation and modern Asians tend to eat less fried food and are cautious about how much salt, butter, ghee and oil they consume. She suggested that her grandparents who are in their 70's and even her parents were unaware of how cooking Indian food in the unhealthy way could give them chronic illnesses.

image of Bollywood actresses several decades ago. In modern Bollywood, actresses are slim, but several decades ago they had voluptuous figures and being curvy was seen as sexy and acceptable.

The trends may be changing in Bollywood, but beliefs back in the UK are much slower to change. My mother still prefers Bollywood actresses many decades ago as they were curvier, which, in her mind, indicated good health, but there is now a question whether the voluptuous frames are returning back to the big screen. Bollywood star and former Miss World Aishwarya Rai, known as the world's most beautiful woman was previously criticised after the birth of her baby as she did not lose her baby fat quickly enough compared to Victoria Beckham who went down to a size zero within a few weeks of the birth of her children. It appears that women in India now want Ashwaria's curves and are even resorting to taking pills to make themselves fat. According to Indian *Vogue* 'skinny is out' and India is celebrating a 'curvy renaissance'.

Another interesting finding from the AHRQ research concerned beliefs about health. Again, I can see the same in my own family. There is a deep-seated belief that health and wellbeing is not in the control of the individual. For example, my mother still believes that ill health is down to bad karma and bad luck rather than her consumption of unhealthy fatty food such as ghee, butter, large amounts of sugar and salt over the years.

Optimistic signs
Things are changing though, and there are some optimistic signs.

Today a vast number of Asians have started to participate in yoga which of course originates from India. An example would be Swami Ramdev, who has gained an incredible number of followers worldwide and has made yoga popular amongst Asians, especially since 2003 when he started to feature on TV with his teachings. Today, he is a popular name in many Asian households around the world as he teaches the importance of yoga and how certain postures can help to control chronic illnesses.

The University of Glasgow also carried out some interesting research in 2013 which suggested that Asians need more exercise than white people in order to reduce the risk of developing diabetes. The results suggested that lower fitness, together with greater body fat in South Asians, explained over 80 per cent of their increased insulin resistance compared to white men.

Through my Asian Exclusive Weightloss Programme, I meet many people who are overcoming and remaking this heritage. I have developed recipes, lifestyle advice, exercise regimes and ways to change the mindset specifically tailored for this community.

It works and it's part of a growing movement for Asian health. The rest of this book introduces this new way of thinking and being and shows how to do it.

I hope you enjoy it, but first I want to let you in on the views of a fellow expert in the field and also tell you the story of one of my clients.

*** An expert's view: Afsha Malik ***

I interviewed Afsha Malik who is the founder of BloominHealth based in Birmingham, and is a qualified pharmacist, exercise and wellbeing specialist and personal trainer. After putting on weight, post-pregnancy, she embarked on her own weight loss and health journey through exercise. Afsha found that exercise gave her a level of health and vitality that no medicine could ever come near and felt the need to share her passion and inspire others that they too can lead a healthy life. Having trained as a personal trainer and then as an exercise specialist she then set up BloominHealth, a fitness company that offers a holistic approach to long-term health and exercise. Afsha works with a diverse clientele in Birmingham and sees people from all walks of life.

Afsha believes that Asian food is, in fact, or at least has the potential to be very healthy as most meals are unprocessed, balanced and there is a good variety of meat and vegetables. The problems are more to do with portion control and lack of nutritional awareness. Home cooking still has a central role in the Asian community and is seen as an important daily task, especially amongst older people who will take time out to prepare fresh meals.

This is good news as traditional cooking skills are more likely to be passed down through generations, ensuring families are less reliant on ready processed meals. However younger generations of minority ethnic groups are more likely to adopt the dietary habits of the mainstream population and therefore experience the same lack of time and cooking skills needed to prepare traditional foods, opting instead for ready made meals and processed food as a quick option. So regardless of ethnicity and culture, the nature of modern living lends itself to unhealthy eating. With the ease of access to processed foods (in shops, supermarkets, fried food takeaways, easy delivery, mobile phone apps), the population in general is fighting a daily battle to try and eat natural, unprocessed and healthy food.

Although Asian food is not unhealthy in itself, the large portion sizes and the lack of awareness of the quantities necessary for a healthy diet mean it can be bad for you. South Asians often live in extended families or enjoy sharing meals together and hence bulk-buy and prepare large amounts of food. This inherently makes portion control quite challenging.

The South Asian population in the UK is very diverse, making it impossible to stereotype a certain type of diet within the community as a whole; some cultures consume high amounts of meat and alcohol, some are strictly vegetarian and teetotal. However, generally the Asian diet is traditionally heavy in starchy staples (rice, chapatti, naan, millet), fruit, vegetables and pulses. Meat and fish are used in curries too. Home cooked foods have less harmful fats and salt than processed foods and are higher in fibre so really, with a little tweaking, the Asian diet is a fantastic option for health.

As a youngster Afsha recalls her mum cooking very simple home cooked Asian food such as lentils, rice, chicken, vegetables and chapattis and they would also mix up the days with having home-cooked western food. They would very rarely go out to restaurants and this was seen as a treat about once a year. Afsha acknowledges that most of us are in a state of confusion when it comes to understanding what is healthy and what is not. There is so much conflicting information out there. Guidelines backed by the food industry, with profits in mind rather than health, have meant years of medical practitioners and governments dishing out advice that has in fact now been linked to the increase in diabetes, heart disease and obesity.

The low-fat, high-carb diet that has now been firmly ingrained into our psyche has led to a massive increase in the consumption of highly processed foods and sugar while reducing natural sources of highly nutritious, high fat products. This information is now coming to light and is recognised by most nutritionists and advisors but changing people's behaviour will take many years.

Afsha is also worried about the research showing that South Asians are at higher risk of heart disease, diabetes and obesity.

Obviously food choices are a factor in these grim outcomes, but there are many other influences: socio-economic background, health inequalities, access to information, cultural and religious beliefs about health and well-being and of course genetic pre-disposition. Afsha says this shouldn't mean we hold up our hands and shun our personal responsibility. In fact, as Asians we have an obligation to ourselves to work harder on our diet and levels of physical activity to maintain good health.

Though Afsha is passionately committed to helping Asians to regain healthiness, she has found it hard to engage many people in this diverse group as they are not willing to make the investment in themselves. Much of her work is now with non-Asians although she welcomes everyone. She feels that in the Asian community there are many complex health beliefs and behaviours that act as extra barriers and prevent people spending time and money getting professional exercise and diet advice. However, this is definitely changing in younger generations as more people begin to adopt mainstream culture, become more affluent and are more health aware.

*** My client's story: Shobana ***

Thirty-six-year old Shobana told me that she was brought up with curries being cooked unhealthily in ghee, butter or oil with high amounts of saturated fat. There was an absence of vegetables and there was a lot of emphasis placed on eating meat.

Shobana points out something very interesting – Indian food and cuisine is complex and diverse. It is not necessarily unhealthy, and she is finding out more all the time.

She says Indian food can be cooked healthily with vegetables and a minimum of saturated fats or cooked unhealthily with high amounts of fat. She now cooks her curries in a small amount of olive oil and her curries are much healthier compared to how her mother cooked.

She also suggested that, when eating out, curries are perceived as 'heavy' as the dialogue amongst friends who would like to lose weight usually involves "How am I going to manage eating well with creamy curries? Don't people always order those crispy samosas? Oh, I love that naan bread!".

Seeing the changes

Shobana argues that it does not have to be this way as there are usually dishes in Indian restaurants that are less fattening such as bhuna dishes which are made with lighter sauces than cream.

She also believes that modern Asians will probably not have any ghee in their household as they are placing more emphasis on becoming healthier, whereas the older generation will always have a tub of ghee in their cupboards. She also suggested that Bollywood actresses like Vidya Balan and Shirmila Tagur are much healthier compared to the models many years ago.

The research carried out by the AHRQ struck a chord with Shobana as it did with me. She agrees that Asians are reluctant to invest money in themselves and especially do not see their health as worth an investment and sees these beliefs amongst her family and friends. However, she is noticing a welcome change. Modern Asians do work out a lot more and take that time out to go to the gym, swimming or exercise groups, although there is still a problem with the older generation.

Like many younger Asians, Shobana has seen her parents suffering with chronic illness made worse by diet. Her parents were both diagnosed with diabetes at just 36 and 37 years of age.

Then there was a cultural clash, as the model of health intervention on offer just did not work for them.

Shobana remembers that medical professionals would write to her parents to offer support to combat their health problems. But her parents found these offers of help intrusive and didn't understand why they were being contacted. Shobana says her parents thought that they knew it all and that they didn't need the help. They would throw all the medical letters away and carry on in the same old way.

Captain in her kitchen
And the attitudes of her parents was not just damaging their health. Their beliefs affected how they brought up their children. She remembers that when she was a toddler, she would be given sugary, milky tea in her beaker instead of plain milk. When she now asks her parents why they did this, they say that the sugar was to add flavour. Shobana now believes that parents should take control of their children's diets and make sure they introduce healthy foods and flavours from a young age.

Shobana suggested that an 'Indian woman is a captain in her kitchen' as she is in control with how the cooking is carried out and how healthy or unhealthy the food is.

Shobana says she has also had to deal with lifestyle issues which affect everyone, not just Asian people, today. Everywhere, people lead busy lives and are more career focused, thus leading to lack of time to cook healthily and look after themselves.

She told me that when she lived in London she struggled to

keep her weight under control as she was busy with her career and would grab fast food and sugary beverages on the go.

Like me, when I was overweight some people preferred her shape then. Shobana also said that when she was slim some people would suggest that she didn't look healthy, and this has been difficult for her to deal with.

Shobana reflects on many of the issues faced by modern Asian women and it is wonderful to see how people like her are taking action and making changes.

***

So, there is some way to go to educate Asians into healthy eating and to invest time and money in themselves, but I have seen many significant changes already in the way young modern Asians are living.

I'm going to be telling you more about their stories in the rest of this book.

*** The experts' view: a new breed of chefs ***

Times are changing. One area this can be seen is in Indian restaurants. I am pleased to see there is a new young breed of chefs that have taken the standard curry house recipes and given them a twist.

Romy Gill, owner of Romy's Kitchen in Bristol simmers lamb to melt away the fat before adding it to a curry. She pan fries her crab cakes rather than deep frying them and has an oil-free chutney on the menu. She does not serve poppadoms in her restaurants as she points out: "Indians don't eat them before a meal".

Chef Ravinder Bhogal believes that British curry houses traditionally catering to the after pub, lager swilling trade are to blame for the unhealthy image of Indian food, with dishes overloaded with cheap oil.

He says: "Food was very healthy when I was growing up at home. But restaurants are changing now, becoming keener to use local British ingredients, more playful, with a lighter style."

Food writer Mira Manek believes that "Indians tend to think curries need sugar, or that onions have to fry in more oil otherwise it won't work, but actually if you use less oil it doesn't matter."

Chapter Two

How we can get to be healthy eaters

Indian food has a reputation for being unhealthy, but it doesn't have to be this way. Ideas are changing and there are many great ways to keep all the taste of food without too much fat and sugar.

There is a common belief that Indian food is bad for you, mainly for the reason that in Indian restaurants it is cooked with clarified butter, creams and such, but like any food, Indian food can be cooked healthily or unhealthily.

The grandparents' generation
As a child I recall my mum cooking a lot of fried food like onion bhajis, samosas, paratha (these are two chapattis stuffed with a filling and cooked with ghee or oil on a pan), cooking curries with clarified butter (ghee) and so on. In my mother's and grandparents generation there was not a great deal of emphasis made on healthy eating so eating fried food and ghee was deemed to be ok as no one knew any better.

My mother is from a large family of seven brothers and sisters and eating healthily was not a priority in her younger days in India as money was tight and there was little awareness of what was good for you and what was bad for you. In recent years there have been more studies that suggest clarified butter and fried food is unhealthy, laden with fat and calories and if eaten regularly they are a heart attack waiting to happen, which is what happened to my father.

When he had his first heart attack we all made some changes to our eating habits, but in my opinion the damage had already been done. My father had an eye for food and would secretly eat Indian sweets, onion bhajis and so on which is where I get my secret eating from.

You need maintenance

As a result I had to change my own mindset so that I don't experience the same health problems.

You have to look after your body as you would look after your car. It requires a lot of maintenance, care and a regular MOT. After all, if you do not look after your body it will eventually break down and stop working just as a car would.

I love food and love the taste of onion bhajis, samosas, Indian sweets and parathas, but I only eat these every now and again as a treat as I know that my health will suffer if I eat them several times a week. I will also become overweight again which is the last thing that I want. I am happy and content with my body.

Being a good guide

However, I still see my family members consuming fat and calorie laden food on a regular basis as they do not have the correct mentality and they do not have the right mindset to make the necessary changes and to eat the right food.

I have tried to guide family members to eat healthily and educate them that clarified butter and fried food is no good for the health, but some usually respond to me by saying, they would rather die happily than to be deprived of the food that they enjoy so much.

Sometimes my mother will respond to me in the same way.

I believe strongly that we must change if we are to avoid the chronic illnesses and premature death which is so common in Asian communities.

Not the only culprit

However, it is not just Indian food that is unhealthy for you. Just like cooking a curry in ghee, English food is bad for you if you cook it in lard.

The traditional English roast, fish and chips and full English breakfast contains thousands of calories and you will get fat if you eat them all the time.

Indian food is healthy if cooked the right way and I am going to share with you how I have changed my cooking style over the years to make my dishes healthier.

Your 1,500 calories in one sitting

Most Indian restaurants cook dishes such as korma, chicken tikka masala, butter chicken with large amounts of butter or ghee and cream and they can contain about 1500 calories per dish. This means you can be going over your recommended daily calorie allowance in just one dish. This does not even include any side dishes such as naan or rice. This is probably one of the main reasons why Indian food is perceived as bad for you.

Foods like poppadums, onion bhajis and samosas are full of fat as they are deep fried, naan bread contains about 300 calories and chutneys can contain a lot of sugar.

The key thing to remember is to be mindful of how much fatty and fried food you are eating and to be aware of how you are cooking your meals or eating out at Indian restaurants. If a dish looks unhealthy avoid it.

At home, creamy dishes such as Korma, chicken tikka masala, and butter chicken can be made much more healthily by cutting out some of the ingredients such as butter and ghee. You can opt for low fat cream or low fat coconut milk to reduce the calorie intake and fat.

The trouble with ghee
Ghee is a form of butter that can be made at home or you can buy it already prepared.

My mother generally makes it at home by melting several blocks of butter in a pan and bringing it to boiling point and allowing it to simmer for about 10 to 15 minutes until it turns slightly golden and develops a layer of foam. The milk solids will sink to the bottom of the pan and she will strain the liquid and store it in an airtight container in a cool dark place. Ghee lasts for a very long time and it will not spoil as the milk solids are removed.

Ghee is made out of pure fat and one 15 gram tablespoon contains about 135-150 calories all of which come from fat. It contains 9 grams of saturated fat or 45% of the recommended daily allowance, and 45 grams of cholesterol whereas conventional margarine contains 1.5 grams of saturated fat and contains 80% less saturated fat. Although fat has some essential properties and we need it for our body to function, ghee has a large amount of saturated fat and is well over the recommended daily intake and if consumed in high doses it can lead to heart disease and diabetes.

Ghee and the guidelines
The guidelines for the recommended daily amount are 70 grams of fat for women and 90 grams of fat for men, out of which 20 grams can contain saturated fat for women and 30 grams for men.

So you can see that just one tablespoon of ghee contains nearly half of the recommended daily intake we are meant to have and this is before the cooking process has even begun. I avoid ghee altogether. Fried food such as samosas, onion bhaji's and spring rolls are also unhealthy for you as they contain a lot of calories and fat mainly due to the cooking process.

If you fry samosas and onion bhajis at low temperatures or put too much food in the pan at one time this lowers the temperature of the oil and lower oil temperatures increases the amount of time to fry the food, thus increasing the amount of fat absorbed during cooking. If you want to eat samosas and spring rolls you are better off baking them which will make them less unhealthy. They are generally made out of potatoes and vegetables and are okay for your health if you change the cooking process.

Dr Justin Zaman, consultant cardiologist and a trustee at the South Asian Health Foundation, suggests that how you prepare food can be as important as what you eat.

"Sri Lankans and Bangladeshis, for example, tend to eat lots of fish, and some Hindus are vegetarian," he says. "These are healthy options, but often the fish or vegetables are fried in ghee, which makes them higher in fat."

Try to replace ghee with healthier cooking oils such as rapeseed oil or olive oil.

Tasty Turmeric

Although you can get turmeric into your system in many ways this recipe is particularly refreshing and tasty.

Ingredients

4 cups of filtered or sparkling water
2 tablespoons of powdered turmeric
4 tablespoons of maple syrup or honey
Juice of 1 lemon or you can add another half if you want that extra kick of lemon
Add the juice of one orange

Method

Mix all of the ingredients in jug and serve with ice if you want it extra chilled.

Medicinal spices

Indian curries are good for you if cooked correctly as the spices that are used have medicinal effects.

Turmeric, also known as golden root, is a common spice that is used to add colour and flavour. When my mother lived in India she would make a paste out of turmeric and oil and apply it to a wound which would heal much faster as turmeric acts as an anti-inflammatory and is great for healing both the inner and outer body. That generation in India were not able to afford medical care or go to the GP so they relied heavily on herbs and remedies at home and often the herbs and spices could be found readily available at home and put to good use. I am a strong believer in alternative healing and am now going to give you some tried and trusted remedies, but if you are sick I do recommend that you also seek advice from your general practitioner.

Home remedies which work

My mother learnt lots about alternative remedies from her mother and she has passed her knowledge onto me. Using herbs and spices for alternative healing still continues many generations on even though there is greater medical care available.

Whenever I catch a cold or have a cough I usually heat up some milk and add about a teaspoon of turmeric, sugar to taste, a small teaspoon of butter (optional) and enjoy this wonderful hot beverage. I feel wonderful afterwards and my cold wears off much quicker and I feel less congested. This remedy can also be used for individuals that suffer from arthritis. The Arthritis Foundation carried out a small pilot study in 2012 and found that turmeric reduced joint pain swelling in patients with rheumatoid arthritis better than anti-inflammatory drugs.

The list of spices is endless and they all have their medicinal values.

If you are feeling sick or nauseous, ginger can be consumed to help alleviate the symptoms. My sister regularly drinks ground

How to make Indian bridal glow mask

**You will need
Chapatti flour
Almond oil
Turmeric**

Mix the ingredients into a sticky paste and apply it to the face like a face mask and leave it on for about 20 minutes.

Remove by rubbing the mixture off with your fingers with a gentle motion which will add to the exfoliation process. Wash the rest of the mixture off and enjoy your fabulous baby soft skin!

ginger added in hot water with a pinch of salt as she can often become nauseous and this helps to relieve any discomfort. I have also tried this and it works wonders.

Garlic can help to lower cholesterol and helps to purify the blood. With all of this in mind, if an Indian curry is cooked correctly it is in effect good for you as the herbs and spices used have such great medicinal effects as well as a wonderful flavour, but it all depends on the cooking process.

Protection from disease and depression
Studies have also suggested turmeric can also aid digestion and can guard against cancer.

According to Cancer Research UK there have been trials that have been carried out suggesting that countries where people consume turmeric at levels of about 100 to 200 grams a day over a long period of time have a lower rate of certain types of cancer.

A 2007 American study found that combining both turmeric and chemotherapy to treat bowel cancer showed that the combination killed more cancer cells than the chemotherapy alone, so sometimes both alternative and conventional medical treatments can work will in conjunction with each other.

Turmeric has also been used to treat major depressive disorders. A new study published in the journal *Phytotherapy Research* has confirmed that not only is turmeric effective in treating depression, it may even be more effective than some of the most common anti-depressants.

Spicing up weddings
Turmeric is also used during weddings as a bridal glow mask. Every bride likes to look fabulous on her wedding day and have the perfect skin, especially Indian brides as they have such big weddings!

My niece got married a few years ago and she had about 800 guests at her wedding so you can imagine how many eyes were on the bride and groom.

Many years ago, before beauty salons were common, the bride would use traditional methods of polishing herself up for her big day. She would apply an Indian bridal glow mask in order to give glowing, radiant skin. During an Asian wedding this tradition still continues even though most brides can now afford to go to a beauty salon.

Spicy savvy: how to make food healthier

1) Use a splash of oil and cook your curry in a non-stick saucepan so that you limit the use of oil. Rapeseed oil is great for cooking as it contains half the amount of saturated fat than other oils. Research has shown that rapeseed oil contains 50 percent less saturated fat than olive oil.

2) If you want to make a creamy curry, such as korma, consider substituting the coconut milk or cream with skimmed milk or cashew nut paste which can be bought from most supermarkets. It will give the same rich creamy taste, but will make it healthier. You might also want to opt in for low fat or light coconut milk. You might even want to try a tomato based sauce rather than a cream based sauce as it is far healthier for you and will cut out excessive calories.

3) Try tandoori style of cooking where you bake instead of frying. Tandoori grilling is the best form of cooking as you will cut out the frying as no oil or minimal oil is used. Using excessive oil or deep frying turns a healthy dish into a fattening unhealthy dish, so avoid deep frying where possible. It is much

Spicy savvy: how to make food healthier

easier to cook the tandoori way and it requires minimal effort and you still get the wonderful flavours from the tandoori.

4) Opt for wholemeal flour when making chapattis and parathas. Some cultures make their chapatti dough by adding oil or ghee to add softness and fluffiness during the cooking process, but this just adds excessive calories and fat. You can still gain the same fluffiness by making your dough in lukewarm water.

5) You may even want to consider using brown rice in your cooking instead of white rice. White flour and rice are made from heavily refined and processed wheat grains, while whole-wheat flour is made from grains that have not undergone heavy processing, so the nutritional value in wholemeal flour and brown rice is far greater than white flour and rice. Apart from white rice looking nicer to the eye in some people's opinion and taking less time to cook there is very little difference in the taste. I love brown rice and the texture of it.

Spicy savvy: how to make food

healthier

6) Try and eat a variety of lentils throughout the week as they are low in calories, contain no cholesterol and are low in fat. Research shows that they have great nutritional value, so you will benefit by incorporating them in your diet. One benefit of eating lentils is lower cholesterol as they contain high levels of soluble fibre. Lowering your cholesterol level reduces your risk of heart disease and stroke. The dietary fibre found in lentils can also help with constipation and digestion. You could try cooking a lentil soup or curry so that you can gain the benefits of these wonderful foods.

Slim and Spicy

Chapter Three

Health, happiness and the modern Asian lifestyle

There is a mood in the air that good healthy food, taking care of yourself and having fun is all important to a happy life. Being slim can give your self confidence a real boost and open up all sorts of new possibilities.

While losing weight has the obvious health benefits, such as reduced risk of heart disease, stroke, arthritis, diabetes and many more, it also has the emotional benefit of increased confidence. You will experience this as you embark on your weight loss journey.

New self confidence
Feelings that you have suffered with because you were overweight may not vanish overnight, but as your body changes and you learn your own self-worth through healthy eating, exercise and a changed attitude, you will find that your self-confidence will increase. Your new healthy lifestyle can be life changing.

As your weight reduces and your body changes, you should find that you stop putting yourself down for being overweight. You should stop feeling self-conscious when you go out, when you are at work or around other people. That feeling of being terrified and anxious in social situations and worrying that you are the fattest person there will go. Just imagine if you lost all of that weight, you would soon love your body and enjoy being around others and they will enjoy being around you because you will give off that positive vibe.

Getting your perfect partner

If you are overweight you often will have little confidence in personal relationships. It can be quite hard to believe that someone would want to be with you.

And there is a truth here. Research suggests that 74 percent of men and 60 percent of women would be uncomfortable dating someone who is obese, according to a study by Jeffery Sobal and Mark Bursztyn.

Improving your relationship

One of my clients, who weighed about 20 stones, had very low self-esteem. She made little effort to dress well, wearing unflattering clothes and she was unhappy with herself.

This had an impact on her relationship sexually and emotionally as she did not want her partner seeing her with no clothes. She really wanted to wear lovely sexy lingerie, but felt too fat.

Once she started to lose weight she felt better in herself and found that she made more effort in how she dressed, avoiding dark baggy clothes and wearing more flattering clothes with some colour. Her relationship improved as her partner complimented her and this made her feel that he really wanted to be with her.

When your partner tells you how great you look, there is no better confidence booster. This should ensure you keep on track and continue to drive your weight loss until you are happy with your target weight.

When you have worked hard to lose weight and get the body that you want, it feels amazing when someone else acknowledges this and compliments you. What better way could there be to keep your confidence and momentum high to keep on pushing your weight loss goal and not give up?

Compliments to motivate you
Whether you are in a relationship or not, a compliment from anyone about your weight loss instantly brings a smile to your face and you should feel that energy and boost right throughout your body. This increases your motivation to charge on.

It gives you the incentive and enthusiasm to drive on until you reach your end goal and get to the size that you want to. When the compliments start coming your way graciously accept them. You certainly earned them with your hard work and persistent attitude!

Slimming sarees

Being slim and willowy is perfect if you want to channel your Asian soul by wearing the most beautiful saree. If you still have some way to go to reach your perfect weight try these slimming tips

Wear light fabrics
Wear smaller prints
Pick slim borders
Wear darker colours
Keep embroidery light
Wear long sleeves

*** An expert's view: India Kang ***

I interviewed Dating and Relationship Coach, India Kang who works with a diverse clientele of women from all walks of life. India gave me her views on whether looks and weight are important in a relationship.

India feels that looks are important for a man in a relationship. She says men fall in love with the eyes and a woman falls in love with the ears.

When you are a healthy weight it signifies you care about yourself, which signals you are likely to care for him too. India mentioned that a man's choice in a partner is reflective of him. He wants to show you off!

He wants a woman to look good on his arm, so being a healthy weight, not necessarily a size zero, is important for men, probably more than for women expecting a man to be slim.

She says that when you make a commitment in a long-term relationship, it's in your interests to look after yourself and remain a stable, healthy weight. She believes that the press and media tell us to be of certain size and that this is unrealistic in the real world, but a balance is good.

***

Better in the world of work

Not only is weight loss good for improving relationships, losing the excess weight could help your confidence at work or if you are seeking work opportunities or going for an important promotion.

Often changes in working circumstances can be a spur for change. One of my clients faced redundancy. She felt it was important for her to lose weight as it would give her the confidence that she needed when attending interviews.

You will be more successful if you lose weight

My client felt fat and had little confidence in herself and what she wore and she was right to lose weight. A survey conducted by the magazine *Personnel Today* interviewed more than 2,000 human resources professionals and the results showed that obese people are discriminated against when applying for jobs, promotions and are more likely to be made redundant – all purely on the basis of their weight. Ninety three percent of HR professionals would choose a 'normal weight' applicant over an obese applicant with the same experience and qualifications.

Just imagine if you lost all of that weight, how confident and successful you would feel at work or when attending interviews. You will dress differently, feel differently and have that sparkle

---

No red lights for Saba

One Asian woman is breaking the mould, by making a success in the male-dominated world of supercar sales.

Preston-based Saba Syed runs one of the country's leading supercar dealerships with her husband. She does the selling and isn't afraid to be a woman in a man's world. In fact, she thinks her gender helps her sell more cars.

And she is slim and glamorous. Think what you could so when that weight comes off. 100 miles an hour ahead.

---

and radiance, because you are on a positive, confident frequency you will give off that vibe. All of the hurdles that could have been in your way previously and kept you from reaching your goals are now becoming much easier to overcome because you feel good and healthy in yourself.

The clothes question

When you are overweight you are like a turtle carrying a protective shell. Most people who are overweight will wear big, baggy dark clothes to disguise their body as much as they can.

Buying clothes in regular shops can be problematic. Usually an outfit in a plus size looks unappealing and unflattering compared to the same outfit in a smaller size.

One of my clients had her heart set on an expensive designer coat, but didn't want to buy it in a larger size as it just didn't look right. She is now losing weight so that she can purchase that coat in a smaller size. A great motivator!

Summertime blues

Some of my clients will have used their weight as an excuse not to do things and to hide who they really are, especially in the summer when they want to go on holiday and wear nice dresses or beachwear.

Summer can always be a difficult time as in most cases you will end up feeling like a beach whale year on year unless you find a way to tackle your weight.

What you want

Just think if you lost all of that weight you could dress how you want and look great when you socialise or go on holiday.

You can emerge as that confident person that you have always wanted to be. You can feel more comfortable in your clothes and when you're on the beach, you can glow with confidence.

When the extra weight is gone, you lose many of the excuses

that you may have used to hide your body and you will find that you dress how you've always wanted to, wearing clothes that flatter your figure rather than hide it. With the weight melting off and your figure emerging under all of that flab, you will find that you are more comfortable wearing the clothes that you have always wanted to get into.

Feeling good

So at the end of this chapter I hope you now have the confidence and motivation to embark on your weight loss journey if you have not already started. If you have started your weight loss journey stick with it and continue to drive it further until you reach your end goal!

Weight loss is not just about vanity, but feeling good both mentally and physically. Lugging all of that weight around is making you unhealthy and slowing you down, it can also have an impact on you emotionally. So start now and you can have the healthy body that you deserve.

Slim and Spicy

Spicy savvy: garam masala, how to make it and what it's good for

Garam masala does not only add flavour to a curry, but the herbs and spices also have great medicinal properties.

My mother makes her own garam masala and when she blends all of the spices together you can smell the aromas throughout the whole house. You only need a small amount in a curry or the flavours can be overpowering. And with even a small amount you still gain all of the health benefits.

Garam masala is made up of a blend of:

Cinnamon (dhalchini). The aromatic spice which has been used for thousands of years acts as an anti-inflammatory and it is also high in fibre. It also helps to control blood sugar levels and has great benefits for people that suffer with diabetes.

Cumin (jeera) helps to stimulate digestion and can also help combat nausea and indigestion.

Dried coriander seeds (dhaniya) can help with digestion and proper functioning of the bowels as they are a good source of fibre. They can also be used to lower cholesterol as well as controlling diabetes.

Spicy savvy: garam masala, how to make it and what its good for

Black peppercorns are also a good source of fibre and a natural metabolism booster.

Cardamom (black elaichi) can aid digestion and relieve heart burn. It can also help to lower blood pressure, increase blood circulation, relieve gas and soothe upset stomachs. If I have a stomach upset I usually chew on this wonderful seed and feel the benefits quickly.

Cloves (laung) can help to support the immune system. They can be used to relive tooth ache by chewing on the seed. My mother usually uses clove oil for tooth aches by dabbing some on a tissue and applying it to her gums. Cloves can also help to prevent the formation of blood clots and help regulation of blood sugar levels as well as reducing inflammation.

Bay leaves are a powerful antioxidant and research has shown that this wonderful leaf can help to prevent cancer, arthritis and ulcers. It can also help in healing wounds.

Spicy savvy: garam masala, how to make it and what its good for

Now that you know the healing power of these herbs here's how to make the masala

My mother adds all of these spices to a big bowl and dries them out for a few days in the windowsill or in the sun if we are lucky to have any. If there is no sun she cooks the spices in a dry frying pan in batches and heats the herbs and seeds over a very low heat for a few minutes, stirring constantly.

As soon as the aroma of the spices begins, she removes the pan from the heat. Drying them out in the sun or heating them releases the aromatic oils from the spices.

Finally she uses an electric blender to grind the spices to a fine powder and she stores the masala in an airtight container ready to be used in every curry. As long as the container is tightly closed it can last for a very long time.

So next time you cook an Indian curry add some extra kick to your recipes with this health-promoting Indian spice mix.

Slim and Spicy

Chapter Four

What causes weight gain and how to reverse it

Junk food, lack of exercise and eating too much are doing all of us damage. But whatever challenges the outside world throws at us we can get back in control. I will show you how over the next few chapters.

There are many factors that can lead to weight spiraling out of control.

These include comfort eating, boredom, weight gained through pregnancy, eating the wrong types of food, consuming too much processed food, and medical-related problems.

Most people with a weight problem have habits where they eat leftovers, eat cakes, biscuits, crisps, have too large portions of food and snack right up to the time they go to bed. Then they feel awful for what they have done when they wake up the next morning.

My Asian clients especially, have an unhealthy diet of fried food or they cook curries unhealthily and then snack on unhealthy Asian snacks such as samosas, onion bhajis, and Indian sweets.

Every time my next door neighbour sees me she will say she cannot stop snacking on sev mumra (an Indian snack with a mixture of spicy dry ingredients such as puffed rice (mamra), savoury noodles (sev) and peanuts every night and she knows it is unhealthy for her. Deep inside the mind of my clients they know they need to eat the right food and exercise to lose the weight, but something within them prevents them from doing it.

Regardless of whether you are Asian or non-Asian, you will gain weight if you eat more calories than you can burn off. And if you cook food unhealthily you will be at risk.

We're all getting lazy

Weight is easy to put on, but it can take a lot of hard work and dedication to keep it off. In an ideal world most people would be a healthy stable weight if they eat and exercise well, but in effect we know that it does not work like this. The obesity crisis is on the rise with more and more people becoming overweight.

In some cases obesity can start from a very young age. It is quite frightening that obesity levels are increasing amongst children. Dr Shahrad Taheri did a longitude study for Action Medical Research for Children to examine the relationship between sleep, health and wellbeing. He found that teenagers between the ages of 11 to 15 who sleep less are more likely to be overweight or obese.

The study found that the teenagers who used devices such as mobile phones and computers the most at bedtime were most likely to be obese and to sleep the least. Figures show that a shocking 17 percent of boys and 15 percent of girls between the ages of two and 15 years are obese in the UK and these figures have tripled over the last 20 years.

You have to question, are parents responsible for what their children are eating and are they laying any ground rules?

I recall growing up riding my bicycle and playing with other children on our street. This happens very rarely now. Many parents use technology to entertain children so they can organise their busy lives in their evenings. This means children are spending more and more time inside.

It is not just children, technology is having an impact on all our health. How many of us sit on our phones or tablets browsing the Internet most evenings instead of getting up and going for a walk or exercising to burn off those calories?

Obesity around the world
I recently visited the USA and I found that a lot of people consume huge portions of food, individuals mainly travelled by car, so didn't get enough exercise.

Although the country is beautiful and there is a lot to see and do, I struggled with the food as I do not eat large portions.

My sister and I found that we shared in restaurants as the portions were far too big for one of us. I also found the drinks were much larger, with a much higher calorie count because of sugar.

Obesity also seems to be rising in India, following a trend in other developing countries.

India loses the food plot
The Indian Times reports that

"Across the board, people are eating less cereals, replacing them with more fat and snacks, beverages and other processed foods ... The only food item that has seen a substantial jump in intake is classified as 'other' in the survey and consists of various hot and cold beverages, processed food like chips, biscuits etc. and snacks. In 1993-94 these made up just 2% of a rural person's nutritional intake but rose to over 7% in 2011-12. In urban areas, this was 5.6% earlier and increased to about 9%."

Unhealthy junk food and processed food has become much more accessible as India integrates into global food markets. Not all households are able to afford these new luxuries, but as the country develops, with rising middle class incomes, fast food consumption is increasing and obesity is rising.

I have visited India several times throughout my life and have noticed that fast food is more readily available. I am pleased to say that most of my family in India have a diet of fresh Indian vegetable curries and most of them have managed to maintain a stable weight. I have also never had curries as good as the ones you get in India as they are so fresh and the vegetables are organic.

Food and energy

I see clients in my practice of all different shapes and sizes. Some clients who come to see me are slim, but they want to change their mindset so they make healthier choices. A lot of junk food usually makes my clients feel sluggish and lethargic even if they are slim.

One of my clients, Mankiran was very slim and looked quite healthy on the surface, but it was only when she came into my practice that I discovered that she felt sluggish and unhealthy due to consumption of junk food and sugar.

She was always on the go and had a very busy working life and relied a lot on sugar and chocolate to help her get through her busy day, working as a consultant.

We were able to change her mindset through hypnosis so that she could make positive changes to her lifestyle and grab control of her sugar cravings. After the session Mankiran said: "I feel more energetic and not dependent on the constant cycle of sugar and chocolate anymore. I feel like I have got my life back and I am back in control."

This lack of control is common. Most of my clients, regardless of ethnicity, come to see me as they have no self-control over food.

Most of these clients make an appointment to see me as a last resort after trying every diet they can think of. They will have tried diets such as drinking smoothies, slimming foods and high protein diets.

The diets have clearly not worked as they are still stuck in the cycle of being overweight. These diets haven't offered them a long term solution to their problems. It will only be a matter of time until they rebel and start overeating again as they want real food. Some end up putting twice the amount of weight back on once they resume a normal diet and leaves them even more miserable and sad than they were before.

*** My client's story: Julie ***

My client, Julie was eating three packets of crisps a day, as well as chocolates. When she worked shifts she would snack constantly on unhealthy food up until bed time. She knew that she had to do something about her unhealthy eating quickly.

Her BMI was already 35. Like many of my clients, Julie had tried fad diets and slimming clubs but she just couldn't keep the weight off.

With just one hypnotherapy and coaching session we were able to address her issues with food and give her a new healthy mind set where she naturally wanted to eat foods that were good for her. It was like a switch that clicked in her mind and made her take action.

Julie has kept the weight off and continues to make healthier food choices which now come naturally to her. She still treats herself to one packet of crisps every now and again, but she generally makes the right choices and most importantly she doesn't feel like she is on a diet.

She still enjoys food, but in smaller quantities. She now knows to stop eating when she is full rather than stuffing herself.

***

Slim and Spicy

Spicy savvy: the way to make the base of a healthy curry

This is usually the base of every curry. You can add meat or vegetables once you have the base. I am going to guide you through cooking a base that can be used in every curry that you cook.

Ingredients:
- 3 chopped onions
- 3-4 cloves of garlic, chopped or crushed
- Thumb sized piece of ginger, grated
- Chilli to taste
- 2-3 bay leaves, optional
- Half a teaspoon cumin seeds
- 1.5 teaspoons turmeric
- Salt to taste
- Half a teaspoon garam masala
- Half a tin of tomatoes or 2 fresh tomatoes

Method:
1.   Add the onions, garlic, ginger, chilli and cumin seeds (bay leaves optional) to 2 tablespoons of rapeseed oil in a pan.

2.   Sauté the ingredients on a low heat, until the mixture turns slightly golden.

3.   Once the onions have browned slightly add the turmeric, garam masala and salt and cook for a further

Spicy savvy: the way to make the base

of a healthy curry

3 minutes on a low heat. The mix might start to stick slightly, but don't worry.

4.   Add 2 fresh tomatoes or half a tin of chopped tomatoes and cook for about 5 minutes, until you get a nice golden texture and you get the wonderful aromas of the spices.

5.   Once you have this wonderful mixture you can add a choice of your vegetables. You can substitute the vegetables for chicken, lamb, fish or even prawns.

6.   If you want a more liquid curry just add some water. You might want to start with a small amount of water first before it becomes too runny.

7.   If you want a creamy curry just add light coconut milk.

8.   Sprinkle some chopped up coriander to season and to add more flavour and colour.

Spicy savvy: the way to make the base

of a healthy curry

This is generally how I cook my curries and they are healthy, with low calories. Plus I gain the benefits of all the spices and vegetables. However, if I added cream, butter or both to my curries I would automatically be making my healthy curry into an unhealthy one, bumping up the calories and fat.

I usually eat my curries with one chapatti or a supermarket wholemeal naan or some brown rice. You can also eat with yoghurt.

Try this simple recipe at home and see how you get on.

A curry is as simple as that!

Spicy savvy: how to cook the

perfect rice

Serves approximately six

Ingredients
- 300g rice
- 850ml water
- 100g peas
- 1 onion thinly sliced
- 1 teaspoon cumin seeds
- Salt to taste

1.   Soak the rice in cold water. You might find that the water is cloudy so keep on rinsing the rice until the water is clear.

2.   Sauté the onions and cumin seeds in a tablespoon of rapeseed oil.

3.   Once the onion starts to slightly change colour add the peas and allow them to become soft.

4.   Once the peas are soft, add the rice.

5.   Add the water and salt, bring to the boil. Once boiled reduce the heat and cover until the rice is cooked.

Spicy savvy: how to cook the

perfect rice

You can add turmeric to add colour and more vegetables if you want to make this into a main meal.

Top tip
To get the perfect rice you always double the amount of water to the quantity of the rice. So if you have 2 glasses of rice you will add 4 glasses of water and so on.
Nutritional value per half cup of rice
Approximately 121 calories,
fat 0.2g,
fibre 0 g,
carbs 26.7g,
protein 2.2g

Slim and Spicy

Chapter Five

Hypnotherapy can help change your mindset

It is not just about what you eat, it is about how you feel about what you eat. The simple techniques of hypnotherapy can tap into your subconscious mind and help you get into a new way of thinking.

We all know that losing weight can be a very long, frustrating and challenging journey. If you are stressed, bored or have low self-esteem it can be even harder to battle weight loss.

If our emotions are all over the place it can be easy to rely on food to make us feel better. This is known as comfort eating or emotional eating. It makes weight loss very difficult and is a cycle that can continue throughout life unless you get help and learn to grab control.

Change how you feel

Most diets and nutrition plans focus on what you eat, but with hypnotherapy for weight loss, you can change how you *feel* about what you eat. If you are on a diet you might eat an apple, but really wish you were eating an apple pie, but with hypnotherapy you might learn to enjoy the apple and not give that apple pie a second thought. This does not mean to say you can never eat an apple pie again, but you will not crave it.

I use the 80/20 rule where 80 percent of the time you eat healthily and 20 percent of the time you are allowed a little of what you fancy. It might be hard for you to imagine yourself eating healthily 80 percent of the time if this is something you are not used to doing, but with weight loss hypnotherapy techniques as well as motivational coaching it is possible to change your thought patterns and gain control over food. And you can allow yourself a little treat 20 percent of the time, such as that apple pie or even a slice of cake. After all we are only human and should be allowed to enjoy food without losing control of it.

I do not ban food
Follow the 80/20 rule and you will feel in control without feeling deprived.

I have followed this myself for at least 10 years and I am a healthy weight. Like an item you are forbidden to touch, eliminating certain foods can make them all the more appealing. If you deprive yourself of the food that you love, you will just want it more and more. The key here is to learn self control and hypnosis can help you to do this.

How hypnotherapy works
Hypnotherapy is a form of deep relaxation and in this deeply relaxed state we are able to tap into the subconscious mind to change behaviour patterns.

The subconscious mind is like a huge filing cabinet that stores all pleasant and unpleasant habits, emotions and visual images. It is not immediately accessible but we can tap into it through hypnosis and change behaviour that we no longer want. Hypnotherapy uses the power of positive suggestions to bring about change to thoughts, feelings and behaviour that are stored in the subconscious mind.

So, hypnotherapy for weight loss is about supporting the subconscious mind to help you make healthier choices with food,

Changing attitudes in India

"There's nothing much to photograph you know," jokes Dr Vanit Nalwa, when asked if she could be photographed in the chamber where she conducts her hypnotherapy sessions. "No candles or swinging pendulums!"

Dr Nalwa, well-known Delhi-based hypnotherapist and neuropsychologist, isn't far off the mark. For many people, the word hypnosis conjures images that have more to do with magic than medicine.

Dr Nalwa, who trained in the UK and has had patients ranging in ages from six to 60, encourages people to try hypnotherapy only if they have an open mind about it . . .

Dr Nalwa, who started practicing hypnotherapy in Delhi in 1996 thinks there's a positive shift. "People are more open and forthcoming and certain techniques are even becoming part of corporate training."

Taken from an article by Reshmi Chakraborty, Hindustan Times, New Delhi to exercise and to motivate you to achieve a fabulous, healthy body. Hypnotherapy can be used to programme your mind so that you have a vision of how good you will look once you have lost weight, giving you that incentive and motivation.

The hypnotherapist will get you to imagine how you will feel with your new look and better health. You will imagine yourself reaching your weight loss goal effortlessly, imagine how energised and confident you will feel and whenever you get the urge to eat something unhealthy, or eat when you're not hungry, imagine not reaching your goal and think about how that will make you feel.

Hypnotherapy is used in India. In bigger cities such as Delhi, Bangalore and Mumbai people are more open to it than the smaller villages. My Asian clients will ask me if hypnotherapy is black magic and if I will cast a spell on them. The answer of course is no. I am not a magician and neither do I practise black magic. I would not know how to! My British Asian clients are more open to hypnotherapy, but the ones who are not can still benefit from my coaching.

Your will is what counts
Hypnotherapy is pleasant and relaxing and there are no side effects with this treatment.

The worst thing that could happen to you is that it will not work for you and you will not take in the positive suggestions given by the hypnotherapist.

We all use hypnotherapy in everyday life, for instance when we daydream or when we lose track of the time. Think of when we're driving and wonder how we got to that destination, this is known as waking hypnosis. I do this all the time and wonder how I got to that place. Daydreaming is also another form of self-hypnosis which we can all go into several times a day.

I get asked all the time if hypnotherapy is a sort of mind control. It is not and no one can be hypnotised against their will. If you are not happy with the positive suggestions that the hypnotherapist gives to you, you will break out of your hypnotic state. No one has ever been stuck in a trance before and not come out.

You will not be in a zombie like state during hypnosis and you will most likely be aware of the surroundings around you. You will not be asleep and you will not be awake, but somewhere in between.

Hypnotherapy is a great tool to help regain control over food rather than let food control you, but it is not a magic wand that will miraculously make you lose weight. The weight loss hypnotherapist will be able to help facilitate the changes, but you will have to take responsibility and put in most of the work. The harsh reality is that if you do not put in the hard work, you will never get the results that you want and you will always remain overweight.

Choose a therapist carefully

If you decide to enlist support from a weight loss hypnotherapist it is important to choose someone that is experienced in weight loss hypnotherapy, and who gets results. It is important that you connect with the hypnotherapist, without this you will not achieve results.

My Asian clients often choose me as I have an understanding of the Indian culture and food. Some hypnotherapists have little knowledge of Indian food so they may not be able to guide you on foods to avoid or how to cook in a healthier way. Your weight loss results will be greater if you enlist support from a hypnotherapist who understands your life and culture. Then it is a fantastic tool to help you to achieve change.

A good weight loss hypnotherapist will help you to regain control over food and should teach you self-hypnosis, so when you are faced with food temptations you know exactly how to handle them in a positive way. They may also give you motivational tools and offer daily contact in order to help you to manage temptation in between sessions.

*** Help yourself at home. Self-hypnosis for weight loss ***

    i.   Find a nice comfortable place where you can relax.

    ii.   Close your eyes and start to relax your muscles from your head down to the tips of your toes. Just imagine all the tension being released from your muscles.

    iii.   Deepen the trance by imagining you are standing at the top of a flight of stairs and you will work your way down the steps. Count down from 10 – 1 and with each step down you will go deeper and deeper into relaxation.

    iv.   By now you should experience a floaty-like feeling.

    v.   Now picture a door in front of you and this is the door to your subconscious mind.

    vi.   Push it open and enter. You might find you are in a garden, beach or lake or wherever your imagination takes you. Find anywhere you will feel relaxed.

    vii.   Start to mentally give yourself positive suggestions like, "I can eat healthy foods now because they taste so much better", "I will no longer eat (whatever unhealthy foods you eat) because they make me feel unhealthy and make me fat, instead I will eat healthy foods because they taste so good", "When I look in the mirror I see someone looking slim and healthy." (keep on visualising the future slim, healthy you).

    viii.   Stay in this wonderful state of positive relaxation for as long as you need and then count back up from 1-5 and open your eyes.

***

Spicy savvy: homemade yoghurt, simple, healthy and versatile

Homemade yoghurt is free from preservatives and free from artificial flavours, it tastes delicious and it is very simple to make even without a yoghurt maker.

Shop brought yoghurts can be heavily sweetened, so making your own can be a good way to avoid the excess sugar. It also contains lots of live bacteria which is great for digestion and your tummy.

My mother makes her own yoghurt, it tastes great and it is so simple to make. In Asian cooking yoghurt is consumed quite a lot. It can be eaten with a curry, used as a marinade, cooked in curries to make a thick gravy and it can also be used to make lassi (a drink made from yoghurt and water or milk).

Ingredients
Serves about 4-5
- 1 litre of whole milk
- 4 tablespoons of existing homemade yoghurt or shop brought yoghurt

Spicy savvy: homemade yoghurt, simple, healthy and versatile

Method

1. Heat up the milk in a large saucepan and bring it to the boil.

2. Once the milk has boiled, turn off the heat and allow it to cool down until it is lukewarm. It could take up to 30 minutes to 1 hour for it to cool down. You might want to dip your finger into the milk for 10 seconds. If it feels uncomfortably hot it is not ready. If it feels warm then it is ready for the next step.

3. Pour the milk into a glass bowl and stir the existing yoghurt into the milk and stir well. Cover the bowl.

4. The final step is important so that the yoghurt sets. You will need to incubate the mixture for about 6-7 hours in a dark warm place for it to set. My mother usually wraps the bowl into a large blanket and allows it to sit in the kitchen overnight. By the morning the yoghurt has set.

Once the yoghurt has set it can be used as a marinade by adding tandoori powder or tikka powder to the yoghurt and left to soak in chicken or your favourite vegetables for a couple of hours until you cook in the oven.

Spicy savvy: homemade yoghurt, simple, healthy and versatile

My mother sometimes adds garam masala, a pinch of salt and grated cucumber to the yoghurt, which is traditionally called raita and it tastes delicious with a curry.

Nutritional value per portion
Approximately 108 calories,
fat 5.4g,
fibre 0g,
carbs 9.7g,
protein 5.3g

Spicy savvy:

how to make a good paneer

Serves approximately eight

Ingredients
- Whole milk
- Vinegar or lemon juice

Method

1. Bring 6 pints of whole milk to the boil and then reduce the heat

2. Add about 2 -3 tablespoons of vinegar to the boiled milk and let it carry on simmering.

3. You will find that the milk will start to curdle.

4. Continue to stir over a heat until it splits completely.

5. Strain the milk in a cheese cloth until there are only cheese solids left

6. To set the paneer, place it on a plate or a tray with a heavy weight on top. I usually place a chopping board on top with a big saucepan of water.

Spicy savvy:

how to make a good paneer

7.   Once the paneer has cooled down and has set you can chop it up into small cubes and add it to your curry base.

If you do not want to set the paneer into cubes you can just add it to your curry base with peas and heat through. I like to add sweetcorn as well as peas, but this is optional. It will look like scrambled eggs, but will taste gorgeous with chapatti or naan.

Nutritional value per portion
Approximately 237 calories,
fat 13.4g,
fibre 0g,
carbs 18g,
protein 12.1g

Spicy savvy:

Sag paneer

Serves approximately three

Ingredients
- 2 onions
- 3-4 cloves of garlic
- Thumb sized piece of ginger
- Half a teaspoon of cumin seeds
- Chillies to taste
- Salt to taste
- Half a teaspoon of garam masala
- 1 teaspoon of turmeric
- 2-3 bags of fresh spinach or 1 tin of spinach
- 3 handfuls of paneer

Method

1. In a saucepan sauté the chopped onions, garlic, ginger, chilli and cumin seeds until you get a nice golden texture

2. Add the turmeric, garam masala and cook for a further 2-3 minutes on a low heat.

3. Add the chopped spinach and let it wilt down.

4. Do not cover the pan as it will release more liquid.

5. Carry on cooking until the spinach slightly dries out.

Spicy savvy:

Sag paneer

6.   Add the paneer chunks and serve.

If you don't have any bags of spinach use 2 tins of tinned spinach.

Serve with yoghurt, chapatti or a wholemeal naan.

Nutritional value per portion
Approximately 194 calories,
fat 10g,
fiber 5g,
carbs 19g,
protein 10g

(Nutritional value per portion in a restaurant)
Approximately 432 calories,
fat 35g,
fibre 10g,
carbs 7g,
protein 20g

Spicy savvy:

Mint chutney

Serves approximately six

Ingredients
- A bunch of fresh mint or 2 teaspoons from a jar
- 250g natural low fat yoghurt
- Half a teaspoon of sugar
- Salt to taste
- Half a teaspoon garam masala
- Chillies (optional)

Method
1. If you use fresh mint blend the mint leaves until they are fine.

2. Add the yoghurt to a bowl with the sugar, garam masala, salt and chillies. Mix the fresh mint in the mixture. If you use mint from a jar add a couple of teaspoons or more if you want it extra minty.

3. Garnish with coriander.
Nutritional value per portion
Approximately 28.5 calories,
fat 0.6g,
fibre 0g,
carbs 3.4g,
protein 2.1g

Chapter Six

Programme your mind: power and motivations

Losing weight means changing your attitude

permanently. You can put yourself in control and get the

lifestyle changes you need by following this programme

of mind exercises and visualisation.

As well as eating in moderation it is important to have a vision of how good you will look in the future once you have shed all of that weight. This will keep the momentum going and your motivation high as it is all too easy to become deflated if the results do not appear as quickly as we want them to.

Try and have a vision of getting into a smaller sized sari, Indian suit, dress or shirt to keep that motivation going. You might even have a holiday planned or a special occasion such as a wedding or a birthday that you want to look good for. Whatever it might be, it is important that you keep an image in your mind of how good you will look when you have lost all of the fat around your body.

Without having a positive mindset and an image in your mind it will be very hard to succeed as it is easy to give up and to get bored on your weight loss journey. The key ingredients to successful weight loss, are a positive mindset, motivation, healthy eating, allowing yourself a treat every so often and exercise. With these, you should be able to keep your weight off long term.

Remember the mind has to be stimulated, otherwise it will get FAT and a fat mind = a fat body.

Why you need will power and motivation in order to succeed
Unfortunately hypnotherapy alone will not help you to lose weight. I often get clients who expect me to wave a magic wand and instantly change their lives in just one session without them putting in any work.

I think it is important to manage the expectations of my clients and to be realistic with them. Then I can help to change your mind set so that you can make healthier choices around food . But all the therapy in the world will not work if you just expect a quick fix and lack the positive mindset and motivation to make changes to your lifestyle.

Achieving your ideal weight should be simple if you apply the tips below. You may encounter some challenges along the way but it is important to keep charging on.

You will need to ensure you have a positive mindset. Have a real look at what you want to change about yourself and then go and get it.

- Be realistic with yourself and what you can achieve.
- Show you are committed to achieving your goal as this results in achieving that goal.
- Without constant commitment and focus, nothing will ever change and you will always be in that eternal cycle of being fat. By having a constant drive you can achieve your ideal weight.
- A positive mindset and motivation = successful weight loss

Some motivational tools
We lead busy lives and have various commitments, but these motivational tools can be incorporated in your daily lives

without taking up too much of your time. These changes are about embracing a lifestyle change which will lead to weight loss and you should be able to keep it for the long haul.

1. Think about the challenges you face with weight loss

Ask yourself what is getting in the way between you and achieving your weight loss goal. Is it money, motivation, emotional eating, time, or lack of willpower? In order to succeed you will need to adopt a can do attitude and think about what actions you need to take to drive weight loss and tackle all of the challenges that are preventing you from reaching your goal. For example, if you do not have time to prepare your lunch in the morning, get up 10 minutes earlier so that you *do* have time. The point is there should be no excuses. If you want something badly enough you will find the time and motivation to do it. I lead a busy life, but I will always find time to exercise and to prepare my meals.

2. Review your actions regularly

Follow the actions that you have put into place to bust the challenges that are preventing you from reaching your goal. These might be waking up early to prepare your meals or making time to exercise. Review the actions regularly and amend them if necessary to ensure you stay focused and keep the new practices in place.

3. Ensure you stay motivated

In order to stay focused and motivated remind yourself regularly of all the things you will do when you are at your desired weight. You may even consider keeping a fat photo of yourself to remind yourself of what you *don't* want to go back to. If I feel I have had a bad week I will look at a fat photo of me and quickly get myself back on track as I never want to go back to being fat again. You might even want to buy a new smaller item of clothing and hang it up where you can see it all the time. This will give you the determination that you will get into it.

4. Confidence booster

Keep reminding yourself of how well you are doing and of your motivation to succeed. Feel your confidence increasing as you keep on proving to yourself that you are in control and that food and fat no longer control you. As you embrace these changes notice your clothes are becoming looser. Remind yourself that you will be able to shop for clothes that you could not previously get into. Notice you have increased energy and you feel less bloated and lethargic. If you have any procrastinating thoughts in your mind tell them to SHUT UP! Fill your mind with a more positive image of you looking slim and healthy.

One bad day does not matter
It is so important that you learn to gain control over food and not let it control and dominate you. Once you get the hang of taking control, your weight loss journey should be much easier. Sometimes we can face situations where we can lose that self-control and resort to food to make us feel better, but then we feel worse after we have stuffed our face. It is important to bear in mind that we are only human and can lose control from time to time, but the key thing to remember is to get yourself back on track and let go of what may have happened with food the night before. Try not to make every day a bad day or you will just turn into a balloon!

Dealing with challenges
We are often faced with challenges with food around Christmas, New Year, wedding celebrations, and parties or even when we go out socially with friends and family as there are so many temptations with food. There are a few key things that you can do to try and help you when you are faced with such situations:
• It is important to remain positive and try not to put yourself down. If you eat a few extra biscuits or an extra samosa try not to feel bad about it. Acknowledge that you have eaten a lot this time and remember not to make the same mistake next time.
• Know what you are putting in your mouth as often the appearance of food can tell you a lot. If it looks unhealthy you

know it contains a lot of fat and calories even though it may taste delicious. Use your common sense and look at the nutritional value of what you are eating if you can. This may not always be possible if you are in a restaurant, although some are now starting to add the calorie content of dishes.

- If you eat a readymade meal, most meals will have the traffic light system on the packaging. Use the traffic light system as much as you can to help you eat right.
- Be prepared for tempting situations and think about how you will handle them. If you are going to a wedding you may want to talk to yourself in your head. Keep on telling yourself: "I am in control and food no longer controls me." Keep on telling yourself that you don't need to eat loads of samosas and onion bhajis. Say you only need one of each to feel satisfied and fulfilled. Remind yourself that they are very fatty and that the fat will sit on your body like lard if you eat too many. You will feel great afterwards for being in control and resisting the temptation.
- Try not to zone out when you are eating. Instead focus on your stomach. If it is getting comfortably full you know you need to stop. So stop overloading yourself even if it tastes amazing.
- If you are going out, try and socialise and chat to people rather than eat. This will help you to control what you eat.

Can you win the food fight?

Yes you can!

You are the only person that has control over your eating habits. You can always resist something if you choose to.

*** My client's story: Baljinder ***

Baljinder, who is just over 15 stones, was on my Asian Exclusive Weight Loss Programme. She had always struggled with her weight, was a typical yo yo dieter and had tried every diet under the sun. She had managed to lose weight, but quickly put it back. She felt she could not carry on counting the calories for the rest of her life, so she went back to her old ways of eating unhealthily.

Before I started working with Baljinder, her diet consisted of eating nothing before she went to work and then at 11am she would eat a sausage cob. At lunch she would eat a sandwich with a packet of crisps or go out at lunch and eat fast food. She would snack on biscuits most of the day. For dinner she would eat 3 chapattis spread with butter and a large Indian curry cooked in clarified butter. Baljinder needed a major wakeup call on her eating as she knew she would encounter health problems soon, (there were already people in her family that suffered with blood pressure, diabetes and cholesterol). She hated being overweight as she was single and felt she would never meet a man. She also felt the pressures of society for her to be a certain size which is a large expectation in the Asian community. Her family were also worried about her health.

I worked with Baljinder to reduce her portions, to halve the amount of chapattis she ate and not spread them with butter, and cook her curries in oil rather than in clarified butter. Baljinder snacked on junk most of the time as she felt low in herself so I worked with her to increase her self esteem and motivation by encouraging her to go for a walk in the evenings when she would be thinking about food.

She enjoyed going swimming so we set a target for her to go swimming twice a week. To motivate her further I asked her to take a selfie of herself and to look at it each time she ate or had the munchies as this would deter her from having that extra mouthful and snacking.

With weekly motivational tools, self-hypnosis and daily texts, Baljinder could see the weight drop off. She struggled with eating less for the first few days as her body was so used to consuming large portions of food, but she found that her body soon adjusted to eating less.

She found that she didn't need to make too much effort to lose weight as she ate her normal food, but cooked it more healthily and less of it. Cutting the unhealthy junk out and limiting it to an occasional treat helped her as we identified she could not live without cakes, so we agreed on her having it twice a week, so she did not feel deprived.

***

Slim and Spicy

Spicy savvy:

Lamb curry

Serves approximately six
Ingredients
- 700 grams chopped lamb leg (although slightly higher in calories, it has a much lower fat content.)
- 4 onions
- Tin of chopped tomatoes
- 3-4 cloves of garlic
- Thumb sized piece of grated ginger
- Half a teaspoon of cumin seeds
- Chilli to taste
- 2-3 bayleaves
- 1.5 teaspoons of garam masala
- 2 teaspoons of turmeric
- Salt to taste
- Water

Method
1.   In a big saucepan add the diced lamb, onions, bay leaves, garam masala, salt, turmeric, ginger, garlic, chilli and tomatoes.

2.   Let the mixture heat through cook for 10-15 minutes.

3.   Add about 1 litre of water. Add more if you want a really liquidy curry, but I usually like a thick gravy. You can add water as you go along.

Spicy savvy:

Lamb curry

4.   Allow the mixture to bubble. Reduce the heat and cover. It can take up to one and a half to two hours to cook through and the lamb will be tender and soft. Garnish with coriander. Serve with wholemeal naan or chapatti or brown rice and salad.

I learnt this recipe from my aunty. It never goes wrong and it is always well liked by friends and family. With this simple method it also means that I have to put in little effort to get such a tasty dish. It also requires no oil or sautéing of ingredients.

Nutritional value per portion
Approximately 375 calories,
fat 15.6g,
fibre 2g,
carbs 10.1g,
protein 34g
Nutritional value per portion in a restaurant:
Approximately 603 calories,
fat 36g,
fibre 6g,
carbs 16g,
protein 56g

Spicy savvy:

Mincemeat curry (keema)

Mincemeat curry or more traditionally known as keema
Serves approximately six
Ingredients
- 500 grams of mince lamb
- 3-4 bay leaves
- 3 large onions chopped
- 3-4 cloves of garlic chopped or crushed
- Half a teaspoon of cumin seeds
- Thumb sized piece of ginger grated
- Chilli to taste
- Tin of chopped tomatoes
- 200 grams peas
- 2 teaspoons of turmeric
- 1 teaspoon of garam masala
- Salt to taste

Method:

1. Add the onions, garlic, ginger and chilli, cumin seeds (bay leaves optional) to a saucepan. Sauté the ingredients in 2 tablespoons of rapeseed oil on a low heat until the mixture turns slightly golden.

2. Once the onions have slightly browned add the turmeric, garam masala, salt and cook for a further 3 minutes on a low heat. The mixture might start to stick slightly, but don't worry.

Spicy savvy:

Mincemeat curry (keema)

3.   Add tomatoes and cook for about 5-7 minutes.

4.   Add the peas and let them cook for a further 5 minutes on a low heat

5.   The key thing here is, in a separate non-stick frying pan add the mincemeat while your base is cooking and let the meat brown. You will notice that it releases a lot of fat and liquid.

6.   Once it has browned, strain the meat and add it to your base and let the meat cook for about 1 hour on a low heat. Garnish with coriander.
You will find that by following the instruction in step 5, your curry will not be greasy. Serve with brown rice, wholemeal naan or chapatti. This also tastes nice with low fat yoghurt.
You can cook spaghetti bolognaise in the same way by releasing the fat in a separate pan.
 Nutritional value per portion
Approximately 303 calories, fat 20g, fibre 2.2g, carbs 12.8g, protein 17.2g
Nutritional value per portion in a restaurant:
Approximately 427 calories,
fat 27g,
fibre 4g,
carbs 17g, protein 30g

Spicy savvy:

Tandoori chicken

Ingredients:
- 1.5kg chicken drumsticks without the skin
- 2 tablespoons lemon juice
- 4-5 tablespoons of low fat natural yoghurt
- Salt to taste
- Chilli to taste
- 2 teaspoon of garam masala
- 2 tablespoons of tandoori spice mix or paste
- 3-4 cloves of crushed garlic
- Grated ginger optional
- Fresh coriander

Method:
1. Mix together the yoghurt, tandoori mix or paste, crushed garlic, ginger, chillies, garam masala and lemon juice in a large bowl.

2. Add the chicken drumsticks and leave to marinade for at least one hour. If you have time you can leave it overnight to absorb more flavour.

3. When you are ready to eat, bake in the oven for 30 minutes to 1 hour turning the chicken regularly or until thoroughly cooked. You should have a nice burnished finish.

Spicy savvy:

Tandoori chicken

4. Finally sprinkle some fresh coriander over the top to give that nice touch.

The lovely succulent chicken can be eaten on its own or with a naan or salad.

You can even follow the same method, but substitute the chicken for fish, lamb or even quorn pieces.

Serve with homemade minted chutney.

Nutritional value per chicken drumstick

Approximately 162 calories,

fat 8.2g,

fibre 0g,

carbs 0.9g,

protein 20g

Spicy savvy:

Chicken korma

Serves approximately five

Ingredients
- 500 grams of chicken breasts or you can use chicken on the bone with the skin off
- 4 chopped onions
- 3-4 cloves of crushed garlic
- Thumb sized piece of ginger grated
- Chilli to taste
- Half a teaspoon of cumin seeds
- 1 teaspoon garam masala
- Salt to taste
- 2 heaped tablespoons of grated coconut
- Coriander
- Tin of light coconut milk
- Tin of tomatoes or use 3 fresh tomatoes

Method
1. Sauté the onions, garlic, ginger, chilli and cumin seeds until the mixture turns slightly golden.

2. Add the turmeric, garam masala and salt. Cook for a further 2-3 minutes on a low heat.

3. Add the tomatoes and cook for a further 2-3 minutes.

Spicy savvy:

Chicken korma

4. Add the chicken to the mixture and once the meat is sealed add the coconut milk and grated coconut.

5. Bring to the boil and reduce the heat. Cover the saucepan.

6. Once the meat is cooked garnish with coriander.

You can add more grated coconut to garnish (optional).

Serve with pilau rice or naan.

Nutritional value per portion
Approximately 306.8 calories,
fat 13.9g,
fibre 2.1g,
carbs 14.1g,
protein 32.5g
Nutritional value per portion in a restaurant
Approximately 623 calories,
fat 24g,
fibre 6.4g,
carbs 33.6g,
protein 96g

Spicy savvy:

Lamb kebabs

Serves approximately five if you have 2 kebabs each
Ingredients
- 450 grams lamb mince
- One finely chopped onion
- 2-3 cloves of garlic
- 1 teaspoon garam masala
- Half a teaspoon of cumin seeds
- Salt to taste
- Chopped chillies
- 1 teaspoon of cumin seeds
- Coriander

Method
1.   Mix all of the ingredients into a bowl

2.   Skewer the meat into long sausage shapes. Alternatively, shape the mixture into small patties.

3.   Barbeque for 4-5 minutes on each side, or until cooked through. Alternatively cook in the oven until cooked.
These can be served in a wholemeal pitta with mint chutney and salad.
Nutritional value per kebab
Approximately 134 calories,
fat 10.7g,
fibre 0.2g,
carbs 1.4g,
protein 7.7g

Slim and Spicy

Chapter Seven

Why fad diets don't work and what to do instead

It is all about balance and eating real food. So

understanding why we need nutrients and caring for our

bodies is important. Taking responsibility and choosing

well is a great feeling and can be permanent.

Lots of people have lost weight successfully through fad diets, but figures show that an astonishing 65 percent put the weight back on. Most clients I see have done this. The problem with diets are that they are not easy to maintain. We crave real food and being on a restricted diet will mean that you may not be nutritionally balanced, and this is harmful for your health.

Diets don't work! I have tried them in the past and have become bored and hungry leading me to eat more! In my opinion the best way to lose weight and to maintain steady weight loss is to have a good nutritional and balanced diet. We are going back to basics, where everything is good for you in moderation.

Short term weight loss can take just days to achieve and is often down to water loss rather than fat. This type of weight loss can be achieved through fasting or very low calorie diets, such as eating only salads and only drinking juices.

However, weight returns very quickly once a normal diet is resumed. Most people will then go back to their old ways, eating large portions and junk food as the mind is not programmed to say STOP once we are full.

Long term weight loss involves a combination of low calorie healthy foods with a treat every now and again and an exercise plan. This type of weight loss can take longer to achieve, but you can keep the weight off. By the time you have lost weight slowly your body and mind has had a chance to adjust to this new healthy way of eating which you should be able to maintain long term.

Why we need nutrients

We need water to break down the food we consume; it also helps to cool the body down and carries away waste. We should drink at least 6-8 glasses of water per day and also get liquids from fruit and vegetables and other foods.

Carbohydrates are a main source of energy and we need that source of energy to carry out our daily activities. Carbohydrates are found in potatoes, pasta, rice, beans, honey and syrup.

Our body needs small amounts of fat which converts to fatty acids, important for cell development. Fat generally comes from meats, nuts and dairy products. But too much saturated fat is bad for you as it produces high levels of cholesterol and this can lead to narrowing of the arteries and heart disease.

Proteins are the building blocks of our body and they are essential in building new cells. Our hair, nails and outer layer of our skin are all made up of protein. Our body can produce some protein by itself, but we must ensure we have a balanced diet of eggs, beans, meats, milk and nuts in order to get the right amount of protein in our body.

According to the NHS, in order to maintain a healthy and stable body a male should consume 2,500 calories per day and a female should consume approximately 2,000 calories per day. We can consume 70 grams of fat out of which 20 grams can be saturated fat, 260 grams of carbohydrates, 90 grams of sugar, 50 grams of protein and 6 grams of salt.

Why we put so much pressure on ourselves

As humans we have a great ability to be hard on ourselves, it is easier to acknowledge our failures than our success. Whether you lose a pound or three pounds a week it does not matter. It is important that you stick at eating in moderation and controlling your portions and forget that dreaded word 'diet'.

When you think about it, if you lost a pound each week you would eventually reach your target weight even if it takes you longer . . . and it is far better than being a pound heavier each week. To achieve successful weight loss it is so important that you adopt a healthy lifestyle where you eat in moderation, exercise, motivate yourself and have patience.

So many of my clients get deflated with losing just one pound a week, but you have to understand that each week will be different and some weeks you may find that you don't lose any weight at all and other weeks you will find you have lost several pounds. Whether you lose one pound or several pounds it is a big achievement and next week you will be at least a pound lighter.

With all of this in mind it is important that you do not punish yourself if you don't lose any weight one week and give up. Instead, notice that you feel more positive, and as the weeks go on you feel more energetic and healthy. Notice you start to make choices with food that benefit you rather than punish you.

I am a strong believer in the law of attraction and maintaining positive energies. With positive thoughts in mind and all the hard work you put in to drive your weight loss you can attract the body and health that you want.

Why yo yo dieters will never lose weight

In all my years of helping people to lose weight I have discovered that the majority of overweight people are stuck in the eternal cycle of losing weight and then have it all pile back on again over a period of time and this turns into a never ending cycle, which is why it is called yo yo dieting.

The major cause of failing to sustain weight loss long term is dieting! Being on a diet covers a huge range of behaviours, such as feeling hungry, feeling deprived of the food we enjoy, getting bored of eating the same food, frustrations with weighing yourself or counting or eating 'special' food, leading you to expect a quick fix. Then you fail because you can't keep up with the diet and you end up believing you will never lose weight.

The typical yo yo dieter will hate the way they look and will decide that they need to take quick action to look and to feel great. They will start off "in the zone" and will manically stick to their latest diet by counting the calories, watching everything that they eat to the last crumb, weighing themselves almost every day and assessing their weight loss at every point that they can. They may be exercising five nights a week and replacing real food with replacement food and they will most likely be denying themselves any treats which will be deemed 'naughty'.

What you will find is that you will lose weight at this point because you are in the 'zone', but then you will start to get bored with your restrictions and the very human instinct of rebelling against denial and deprivation will kick in. You may have had a stressful day at work or at home so you fancy a night in front of the TV rather than down at the gym. Whilst in your relaxing zone you start to eat the odd 'naughty' thing and this turns into a more regular habit and you slowly start to break the rules. Over a period of time you end up going back to your old behaviours.

You end up going back to hating the way you look so you decide you must take action once again, you fail and this miserable cycle rolls on. Most will carry on like this, I see it all the time.

Stopping the excuses
In my practice I do not teach my clients to diet. It is not about the black and white thinking of either being on a diet, or eating for England. It's all about balance. We go back to basics where everything is good for you in moderation.

That's why my approach to weight loss makes so much sense as my clients will still lose weight without being on a rigid diet. In my practice the word 'diet' is banned as I do not agree with them. There are definitely no quick fixes. I do not ban naughty foods as everyone has a weakness whether it is cakes, crisps, chocolates, eating out or getting a takeaway every so often. My client Julie loved crisps so she now eats one packet of crisps a week rather than three or four packets a day which she used to eat. I teach clients to eat everything and anything, but with a sense of balance.

Weight loss is all about facing up to your food demons and stopping the excuses that keep you fat, so rather than eat the whole biscuit tin, have one or two that will keep you satisfied and fulfilled. This is better than not having any at all (then you will feel deprived) and it is better than having the whole tin. Eating with a sense of balance will help you to achieve much better weight loss results than being on a rigid diet.

Eat regular meals
It is important that you have three balanced meals a day and two healthy snacks in order to achieve weight loss. In order to maintain weight loss, live 80/20 for the rest of your life where 80 percent of the time you have healthy balanced meals and 20 percent of the time you allow yourself room for a little of what you fancy like a takeaway, going out for a meal, a slice of cake or whatever it is that satisfies your taste buds.

A lot of people that I come across believe that skipping meals will help with weight loss as you are reducing calories that you consume, but it is important that you eat regularly throughout the day and don't skip meals as your body will go into starvation mode and will begin to burn lean tissue and muscle as a fuel source, so if you do not eat enough you will lose the wrong type of fat and this is harmful for your health.

We all lead a busy hectic life and things can get too much from time to time, and poor planning can lead to us not being bothered to cook or to eat well. This is when things with our weight can get out of control because you will eat anything that you can to fill the stomach and in most cases it will be something unhealthy. By the time we know it we have piled on the pounds as we have not planned ahead to fit food into our busy life. This may not always be easy to do, but there are some easy tips that you can follow.

*** Help yourself: good planning ***

1.   Try and plan what you will eat for the week. It's when we don't plan we can eat rubbish which makes us pile the weight on. This will help you to control what you eat and to avoid quick options such as fast food and an unhealthy takeaway.

2.   Think about your plans for your day. If you are short on time don't pig out on junk food, try and cook something quick and healthy like Indian vegetable rice or a stir fry. Have ingredients ready to hand. A stir fry will probably take the same amount of time to cook as having a takeaway delivered.

3.   Make sure you have done your weekly shopping and have healthy ingredients to hand i.e. plenty of vegetables, meat and fish. Some of this can be frozen.

4.   You can cook in bulk and freeze it for the week. You could cook an Indian curry and freeze it in takeaway containers. You can take it out the night before and let it defrost overnight. The curries can be kept in the freezer for some time before they spoil.

Preparing and planning will help to keep your eating in check and you will find that you will feel better and healthier as the weight starts to fall off.

***

Eat less later

In order to have successful weight loss you should be eating like the saying: breakfast like a king, lunch like a prince, and dine like a pauper.

Breakfast is exactly what it says, breaking your fast, and for most people the time they spend in bed is the longest period they go without food. Your body needs to refuel after hours of sleep. Eating breakfast will ensure your blood sugar levels are back up and ensure your brain is functioning properly and will help with concentration and give you that kick start. In short breakfast will set you up for the day. Breakfast is the one meal that you can pack in some carbohydrates since they give you energy and you will burn them off throughout the morning, so ensure you eat breakfast if you want to lose weight. Some believe that skipping breakfast will help them to lose weight, but you will miss out on important nutrients and are more likely to eat more food than usual at the next meal or nibble on high calorie, fatty snacks to starve off hunger.

If you do not have time to eat breakfast in the morning, you might want to keep your breakfast at work or plan your day ahead where you wake up earlier so that you *do* have time to eat. Planning and preparing your meals will help you to focus and will help to keep you on track of what you are eating. You might want to try breakfasts that keep you full for longer such as porridge, muesli, scrambled or poached egg on toast, granola or low fat yoghurt.

Balance is all

For lunch, eat a substantial meal to fuel you for the afternoon but make sure that it isn't too heavy. Essentially, it should be a medium-sized meal – smaller than breakfast but larger than dinner. Lunch is just as important as breakfast. How many of you survive on just a coffee and a snack bar for lunch? Just like breakfast, lunch provides us with the energy levels to get us through the rest of the day without pulling on the body's reserves. If we skip lunch we become irritable, sluggish and will most likely lose concentration.

If I skip lunch it makes me sluggish and irritable and it takes me several hours to get my energy back.

You should be eating lunch around four to five hours after breakfast. If you leave eating lunch for too long your body will become over hungry. This can lead to picking and snacking on high sugar and fatty foods such as crisps and chocolates to get the energy back. Apart from pilling on the pounds with these high fat snacks, these foods provide little or no nutritional value compared to real food.

For lunch try to eat whole grain sandwiches, pasta, lentils or beans as they keep you full for longer. If you become hungry in between meals have some chopped up fruit or vegetables which are low in calories and fat. Chewing your food properly and not wolfing it down is also important as it helps with digestion and stops bloating.

Lastly, it only makes sense to eat a well-balanced smaller meal for dinner because you have less time to work it off and will store any extras as fat when you go to bed. If you eat right throughout the day, you should be satisfied with this "pauper" sized meal.

*** My client's story: Gurminder ***

Gurminder was on my Asian Exclusive Weight Loss programme and has made amazing progress. She has dropped almost two dress sizes and is still losing weight.

Gurminder had battled with her weight for the majority of her life, particularly with sugar cravings and controlling her portions. Her biggest weakness was cakes and chocolates and she would eat for the sake of eating rather than because she was hungry. She had tried fad diets in the past which had demotivated her as then she would move onto the next best diet to try and shift the weight and fail again.

Gurminder works out several times a week and makes a 35-minute walk to work every day, so she should be slimmer, but she was eating more calories than she was burning off. Most days she would exercise and then eat an unhealthy large portion of food afterwards and she would know deep down that there was no point in having done any exercise. Her food issues needed to be addressed so that she could have the slimmer, healthier body that she has always wanted. Most importantly she wanted to feel sexy and not have the worry of any health issues that could present in later life.

I identified a treatment plan that would work for Gurminder. She is a very active lady so we didn't need to work on incorporating any exercise; she needed a major reality check on her eating habits. Through combined coaching and hypnotherapy I was able to reframe her mind so that she would eat smaller portions, cook her Indian food healthily and plan her lunches which were having a big impact on her weight. She was given an Asian exclusive 80/20 menu plan where 80 percent of the time she ate healthily and 20 percent of the time she was allowed a little of what she fancied. This meant that she did not have to deprive herself. The menu plan gave her guidance on using healthy ingredients for cooking and recipe plans which could be incorporated in everyday life.

With mind programming techniques, coaching and self-hypnosis Gurminder was able to eat less and stop when she was full. She was given different motivational tools each week to drive her weight loss and to keep her enthused. She bought a smaller Indian outfit that she would eventually be able to get into and visualised how sexy and slim she would look once she has lost the weight. She knew that motivation was a key aspect to keep her drive going, so she received daily text messages from me to monitor her progress and to keep her momentum high.

***

Slim and Spicy

Spicy savvy:

Cauliflower and potato curry (and other vegetables)

Cauliflower and potato curry (you can add any other vegetables to this dish)

Serves approximately six

- 1 cauliflower cut into bite sized pieces
- 2 potatoes chopped into medium squares
- 2 large onions chopped
- 3-4 cloves of crushed garlic
- Thumb sized piece of ginger grated
- Chilli to taste
- Bay leaves optional
- Half a teaspoon of cumin seeds
- 1.5 teaspoons of turmeric
- Salt
- 1 teaspoon of garam masala
- 2 fresh tomatoes or half a tin of fresh tomatoes

Method:

1.   Add the onions, garlic, ginger, chilli, cumin seeds (bay leaves optional) to a saucepan. Sauté the ingredients in 2 tablespoons of rapeseed oil on a low heat until the mixture turns slightly golden.

2.   Once the onions start to brown add the turmeric, salt and garam masala and cook for 2-3 minutes.

Spicy savvy:

Cauliflower and potato curry (and other vegetables)

3.   Add the potatoes and cook on a low heat for 5-7 minutes.

4.   Add the cauliflower and tomatoes and cover until cooked.

5.   Garnish with coriander.
Serve with yoghurt, chapatti or a wholemeal naan and salad.
Nutritional value per portion
Approximately 156 calories,
fat 6.2g,
fibre 5.9g,
carbs 23.6g,
protein 4.3g

Spicy savvy:

Tomato curry

Serves approximately four
Ingredients
- 2-3 bayleaves
- 2 onions sliced
- Half a teaspoon cumin seeds
- 3 cloves of garlic
- 1 teaspoon of turmeric
- Salt to taste
- 1 teaspoon garam masala
- Chilli to taste
- About 650 grams tomatoes sliced in wedges (can use any mix of tomatoes)
- Half a teaspoon of brown sugar (optional)
- Chopped coriander

Method
1.   Heat the oil in a large saucepan and add the bay leaves, onion, garlic and chilli. Sauté for a few minutes.

2.   Add the cumin seeds, turmeric, garam masala and salt and cook for 2-3 minutes

3.   Add the tomatoes and sugar and cook for 10 minutes on a low heat until the tomatoes are soft.

4.   Garnish with coriander

Spicy savvy:

Tomato curry

This quick and easy tomato curry is so simple and can be eaten with wholemeal chapattis, naan, brown rice or even as a chutney.
Nutritional value per portion
Approximately 60 calories,
fat 0.4g,
fibre 2.3g,
carbs 13.5g,
protein 2.4g

Spicy savvy:

Lentil curry

Serves approximately four
Ingredients
- 200 grams red lentils
- 300ml water. You may need more if you want a less dry curry.
- 1 chopped onion
- 1 teaspoon cumin seeds
- 2-3 cloves of crushed garlic
- Thumb sized piece of ginger grated
- Chilli to taste
- Salt to taste
- 1 teaspoon garam masala
- 1.5 teaspoon turmeric
- Bayleaves (optional)
- Coriander

Method:
1. Rinse the lentils under cold water until the water is clear.

2. In a large saucepan add the lentils, turmeric, salt and water and bring to the boil.

3. Loosely cover, reduce heat and simmer for about 20-30 minutes, stirring often until the lentils are soft. You should have a slightly thick texture.

Spicy savvy:

Lentil curry

4.   In a separate pan add the onions, ginger, chilli, garlic, bayleaves and cumin seeds, in a little rapeseed oil and sauté on a low heat until the mixture turns golden.

5.   Add the garam masala lastly and cook for a further 2 minutes.

6.   Finally pour the sizzling hot mixture into the lentils, stir and garnish with coriander.

You can add chopped tomatoes if you wish.
Serve with boiled rice and salad or wholemeal chapattis or naan.
Nutritional value per portion
Approximately 70 calories,
fat 0.2g,
fibre 2.1g,
carbs 12.3g,
protein 4.2g

Spicy savvy:

Indian spiced cauliflower rice

Serves approximately five
Ingredients
- One cauliflower grated
- 1 teaspoon of turmeric
- 1 teaspoon cumin seeds
- 1 teaspoon of mustard seeds
- 1 teaspoon garam masala
- Chilli to taste
- Thumb sized piece of ginger grated
- 3 cloves of crushed garlic
- 4 spring onions chopped
- Salt to taste
- 2 handfuls of peas
- Coriander

Method
1.   Break the cauliflower up into florets and put into a food processor and whiz until the pieces have broken up and look like rice.

2.   Heat up the rapeseed oil in a large pan and add the garlic, chilli, ginger, cumin seeds, mustard seeds, bay leaves, spring onions and fry on a low heat for 2-3 minutes.

3.   Add the turmeric, garam masala and salt and cook for a further 2 minutes.

Spicy savvy:

Indian spiced cauliflower rice

4.   Add the peas, cauliflower and 2 tablespoons of water and stir through.

5.   Cook for 10 minutes on a low heat or until the cauliflower has cooked through.

6.   Garnish with coriander.

This can be served on its own or with mint chutney.

Nutritional value per portion

Approximately 110 calories,

fat 1.2g,

fibre 6.4g,

carbs 12.3g,

protein 4.9g

Spicy savvy:

Chickpea, spinach and potato curry

Serves approximately six

Ingredients:

- 2 chopped onions
- 3 cloves of crushed garlic
- Thumb sized piece of ginger grated
- 1.5 teaspoon of turmeric
- Salt to taste
- 1 teaspoon garam masala
- Half a teaspoon cumin seeds
- Chilli to taste
- 1 large potato chopped into medium sized squares
- 1 bag of spinach
- 2 tins of chickpeas drained
- Half a tin of tomatoes or 2 fresh tomatoes chopped
- Chopped coriander to garnish

Method:

1.   In a large saucepan sauté the onions, garlic, ginger, chilli and cumin seeds in some rapeseed oil until the colour starts to turn slightly golden.

2.   Add the turmeric, garam masala and salt and cook for 2-3 minutes.

3.   Add the tomatoes and cook for a further 3-4 minutes until you get a nice golden texture.

Spicy savvy:

Chickpea, spinach and potato curry

4. Add the potatoes and cook for a further 10-12 minutes on a low heat with the lid on.

5. Add the chickpeas and about 500ml of water and bring to the boil.

6. Reduce the heat and cover the saucepan.

7. When the potatoes are nearly cooked add your bag of washed spinach and cover the pan until everything is cooked.

8. Garnish with coriander.
Serve with brown rice, chapatti or naan and salad.
Nutritional value per portion
Approximately 150 calories,
fat 2.8g,
fibre 5.7g,
carbs 23.8g,
protein 6.5g

Spicy savvy:

Bombay potatoes

Serves approximately five

Ingredients

- 4 -5 large potatoes chopped into small squares
- Chilli to taste
- 2 teaspoons of mustard seeds
- 1 teaspoon of cumin seeds
- 1 teaspoon of garam masala
- Salt to taste
- 1.5 teaspoons of turmeric
- Half a teaspoon of coriander seeds
- Garnish with coriander

Method

1. Heat up some rapeseed oil in a pan and add chilli, mustard seeds and coriander seeds and cook on a low heat for 3-4 minutes on a low heat.

2. Add the turmeric and cook through for about 2-3 minutes.

3. Add the potatoes, salt and garam masala and stir through until the potatoes are covered with the mixture.

4. Cover the saucepan and stir the potatoes regularly as they may stick.

Spicy savvy:

Bombay potatoes

5.   Once the potatoes are cooked through garnish with coriander.

Serve with naan or chapatti and some homemade yoghurt.
Nutritional value per portion
Approximately 174 calories,
fat 4g,
fibre 2.8g,
carbs 32.3g,
protein 2.8g

Spicy savvy:

Kidney bean and sweet potato curry

Serves approximately six

Ingredients
- 2 chopped onions
- 3-4 cloves of crushed garlic
- Thumb sized piece of ginger grated
- Chilli to taste
- Half a teaspoon of cumin seeds
- 1 teaspoon of garam masala
- 1.5 teaspoons of turmeric
- Salt to taste
- Half a tin of tomatoes or 2 chopped fresh tomatoes
- 2 tins of kidney beans drained.
- 2 sweet potatoes chopped into cubes
- Garnish with coriander

Method

1.   Sauté the onions, garlic, ginger, chilli and cumin seeds in some rapeseed oil until you get a nice golden texture.

2.   Add the turmeric, garam masala and salt and cook for a further 2-3 minutes on a low heat.

3.   Add the tomatoes and cook for a further 2-3 minutes.

4.   Add the sweet potato and heat through for 3-4 minutes.

Spicy savvy:

Kidney bean and sweet potato curry

5.   Add the kidney beans and about 1 litre of water.

6.   Bring to the boil and reduce heat and cover the saucepan.

7.   Once cooked garnish with coriander.
Serve with brown rice or wholemeal chapatti.
Nutritional value per portion
Approximately 266 calories,
fat 2.1g,
fibre 6.7g,
carbs 28.4g,
protein 31.5g

Spicy savvy:

Paratha

Paratha
Serves about 5
For the filling you can either have potatoes, carrots, cauliflower, and white radish. I'm going to show you how to make a potato paratha

Ingredients
- 3-4 potatoes
- 1 large onion finely chopped
- 1 teaspoon garam masala
- Half teaspoon cumin seeds
- Coriander
- Mint (optional)
- Salt to taste
- Chilli to taste

Method
1. Microwave the potatoes so that they are soft enough to mash.

2. Peel and mash the potatoes.

3. Mix the onion, chilli, garam masala, cumin seeds, salt, coriander and mint with the potatoes.

4. You will have a nice fluffy potato mixture.

Spicy savvy:

Paratha

For the dough
- 500 grams chapatti flour
- Water

Method

1. In a wide bowl add flour and required water, mix well and knead until you get a nice firm dough.

2. Let the dough set for about 20 minutes and then knead it again.

To make the paratha

1. Roll out 2 small chapattis

2. Spread the potato filling in one rolled out chapatti and cover with the other. Press around the edges to ensure the filling doesn't come out.

3. Roll again until it's about 3mm thick.

4. Cook on a pre-heated pan on a low heat turning regularly until both sides are golden brown.

5. You can add oil on both sides should you wish but this could make it unhealthy.

Spicy savvy:

Paratha

Serve with yoghurt.

If you want to make a paratha with white radish, carrots or cauliflower all you have to do is grate the ingredients and add the onions, garam masala, salt, chilli, coriander and cumin seeds. You may find that the mixture releases a lot of liquid once the salt is added so you may need to drain some of the liquid to prevent the paratha from becoming soggy.

Nutritional value per portion
Approximately 162 calories,
fat 5.5g,
fibre 2.8g,
carbs 36.5g,
protein 4.6g

Slim and Spicy

Chapter Eight

Exercise for health and weight loss

Exercise will speed up your metabolism and help you lose weight. There is also increasing evidence that it is good for you mentally and will protect you against a whole number of chronic illnesses.

Exercise is a normal part of my daily life and comes naturally to me, but this is the experience of the minority of Asians in the UK, particularly with the older generation. For the majority of Asians, exercise is not deemed to be a priority and is undervalued.

I see a lot of friends and family who do not incorporate exercise at all in their daily lives and continue to eat unhealthy food. They would much rather sit at home watching television than to get up and get fit and active. It is no wonder chronic illnesses such as type 2 diabetes and cardiovascular disease are common amongst this group.

When you ask most Asians the reasons for not doing any exercise, they will respond with excuses about not having time, work commitments, family, boredom or having little motivation.

I find most people respond with the same answers regardless of culture, but in the Asian community there are more complex, deep-rooted cultural challenges which make it harder to overcome these barriers.

Studies have shown that Asians lack understanding of the relationship between lifestyle and disease. Many who have a lifestyle-related condition were unconvinced of the impact their lifestyle choices had on their health. Those with a health condition fail to take advice from health professionals to change their lifestyle even if they are recommended exercise. In addition being overweight has been seen as representing good health. I have witnessed these things amongst my friends and family.

Protect your health

Regardless of ethnic group it is important to exercise as it can reduce your risk of major illnesses such as heart disease, type 2 diabetes, stroke and some cancers. Whatever your age or ethnic background, everyone should incorporate some daily exercise. Exercise can also boost self-esteem, mood, sleep quality, reduce stress, depression and studies suggest it even lessens your chances of developing Alzheimer's disease.

According to NHS guidelines, 19-64 year olds should be doing 150 minutes of moderate aerobic activity such as cycling, fast walking, water aerobics or lawn mowing every week. This equates to about 21 minutes of physical activity per day. Along with moderate aerobics you should do strength exercises on two or more days a week such as biceps curl, weight lifting or even gardening, which works all of the muscles in your body.

Or you could do 75 minutes of higher aerobic activity a week such as running, swimming fast, singles tennis or aerobics. This should be combined with 2 or more days of strength exercises. Or you can do a combination of the 2 options above. For more information on exercise guidelines you can visit the NHS website.

Exercise increases the number of calories you burn, this will speed up your weight loss and get results much quicker. Plus, you build muscle, which keeps your metabolism in high gear.

One of my Asian clients Gurminder would walk for 30 minutes daily, go to the gym about 3-4 times a week and do cardio, but she had a poor diet. The exercise she was doing weekly, which was more than most people, did not affect her weight. She justified her unhealthy eating by saying she exercises regularly, but I quickly identified that doing the amount of exercise she was doing was a waste of time as her eating was so poor.

I would tell any client that you have to eat healthily and exercise in order to achieve successful weight loss. In other words, if you have had a fantastic workout and then you go home and have a massive unhealthy takeaway then your exercise will have been a waste of time. You will consume more calories than you will have burnt off. It's about finding a balance so that you can enjoy food without putting on tons of weight.

Do what you enjoy

It is important that you find an exercise that you enjoy doing. You might want to think about joining a gym, Zumba classes, swimming, aerobics, bhangra aerobics which has become popular, join a step class, yoga or whatever it is that you enjoy doing.

As long as the exercise gets your heart pumping and you work up a sweat it is good for the health. You might even want to find an exercise DVD if you are stretched for time. If you are not able to exercise, try and take a brisk 30-minute walk every day. If you struggle to do this daily start by walking two times a week and slowly build it up to more. If you are not able to get out, walk a few laps around your garden. Try not to make exercise a tedious chore so find something that you enjoy doing. Some of my friends and family have created a walking group where several of them will take a brisk walk together and this also gives them a chance to socialise and catch up with one another. Try and make exercise enjoyable and sociable if you can. Then you will look forward to it and will want to do it.

If you want a healthy, slim body then it needs to be maintained. Just like if you don't maintain your car, there is an increased possibility that it will stop working. Similarly, if you don't exercise your body, it will slowly stop working the way that you want it to. So start exercising now before it is too late.

Ease into exercise

If you are new to exercise or you have had a break from exercise for some time ensure you speak to your doctor, nurse or personal trainer regarding an exercise plan that is suitable for your needs.

Depending on your weight, health and how active or inactive you have been in the past, you may need to ease into it slowly and then build it up as you start to do more. Once you have got more active you can incorporate more activity into your daily life.

Here are a few tips on what you can do now in your daily life:

- If you always take the lift, try and use the stairs even if you work on the furthest floor.
- If you drive, park further away from your destination so that you have to walk a bit.
- If you usually eat your lunch at your desk, take a 10 to 20 minute walk first, then have your lunch.
- Instead of watching TV at the weekend or evenings and reaching for those snacks, plan active pursuits where you won't think about food. You might think about going to the park for a walk or go around the block, go swimming or find anything that you enjoy doing. The idea is that you don't sit there thinking about food.
- Try and think about joining an exercise group, whether it is the gym, Zumba, bhangra classes, step or yoga. If you are not able to there are lots of exercise DVD's on the market to choose from.
- Aim for 30 to 60 minutes of continuous aerobic activity, such as swimming, cycling, walking, dancing or jogging at least three times a week. If you are new to exercise start slowly and then build it up.

Whatever exercise plan you decide on, it's a good idea to set weekly goals and achievements to keep the focus going. Try and write down what activity or activities you plan to do, on what day of the week, for how long, and at what time of day. Be as specific and realistic as possible. For instance, write down "Tuesday: Walk for 20 minutes at 7pm to the park and back. If this is the only thing that you can achieve this week don't worry. You can work on achieving more the following week.

At the end of each week, review your goals and set new ones for the following week and again be realistic.

Research shows that setting goals will help you stick to your programme. It will clarify what you're supposed to do and let you track your progress. If you hit a roadblock later on, you can refer to what has worked in the past, or use your accomplishments to re-energise yourself.

*** *Expert opinion from Afsha Malik* ***

In the earlier chapter I talked about Afsha Malik, Exercise and Wellbeing Specialist and Personal Trainer. Afsha suggests that exercise is one of the most important pillars of health. Exercise has been described as a magic pill - if all the benefits that exercise offers could be formulated into one pill, we would be paying a lot of money to get our hands on a supply. Yet it is freely available for us to access ourselves whenever we want. All we have to do is turn up!

Sustaining a long term exercise program is crucial in weight management. Obviously exercise helps with weight loss to an extent, but what is even more important is to establish a daily program of moderate exercise to keep weight within a healthy range. A balance of different types of exercise is recommended including aerobic, strength training and flexibility. Often amongst women, strength training is neglected and yet this is probably the best way to improve metabolism as we get older.

I think the Asian community in the UK have many barriers to exercise. It's not so much that it is undervalued but perhaps more under-prioritised. Levels of physical activity in the South Asian community have been shown to be amongst the lowest in the UK, especially within the female population. Although most people are aware that exercise is beneficial and there is a latent desire to do more exercise, the numbers show that people are just not changing their behaviour. Reasons are complex; immigration, social class, health inequalities, deprivation, access to facilities, language barriers, family commitments, cultural and religious beliefs and so on. The younger generations are definitely accessing services more widely than the first generations

***

*** My client's story: Anita ***

Anita was 14 stones and was very unhappy with her body. She had low self-esteem, felt sorry for herself and used food to make herself feel better and to distract herself from other things in her life.

Anita knew that her emotions dictated how she ate, how much she ate and what she ate. She felt horrible each time she looked in the mirror and felt like a fat ugly thing as she could not get into any of her old clothes and felt self-conscious each time she went out. Furthermore, she made no effort on her appearance, would wear little or no makeup and would hardly straighten her hair. She felt there was no point because she felt too fat.

Anita was eating large portions of food, and had no routine, she would skip breakfast and would eat chocolates, cakes, biscuits, peanuts, crisps or anything she could get her hands on. Some days she would be eating five packets of crisps a day! When we explored her routine with food, Anita said she has five bad days in the week and only two good days of what she called healthy eating. When she said this out loud she knew she had to do something about her weight quickly or she would get fatter and fatter.

She was in despair and felt hypnotherapy was her last resort because she had tried everything else and nothing had worked. I put her on my Asian Exclusive Weight Loss Programme to show her exactly how she can regain confidence and be slim once again.

Anita was given my Asian exclusive 80/20 menu plan which was achievable and this would keep her eating in check. She was given weekly tools so that she could keep herself motivated in between sessions.

These included sticking up warning signs on her treat cupboards, a selfie of herself to deter her if she felt like binging and a smaller item of clothing that she would eventually be able to get into.

We did weekly hypnosis and I got her to visualise what life would be like when she lost the fat. I also got her to detest fat and see it leaving her and her slim body appearing from underneath.

Anita was also given daily motivational texts and offered a 24 hour SOS service so that she could get in touch with me if she felt like giving up or needed that extra support.

Anita saw the weight coming off. She is still losing weight and she plans to celebrate by getting some new clothes when she has reached her target weight.

Working together to achieve a healthier mind and giving that inspiration and motivation makes a huge difference in reaching weight loss goals faster. It worked for Anita and it can work for you.

***

Slim and Spicy

Chapter Nine

Healthy eating the Asian way, by the experts

Jevanjot Kaur Sihra is an experienced Registered Dietician.

She spoke to me about making the Asian diet healthy and

what good nutrition means.

Jevanjot Kaur Sihra, an experienced Registered Dietician has contributed chapters in the *Multicultural Handbook of Food, Nutrition and Dietetics* by Aruna Thakur and the *Manual of Dietetic Practice* by Briony Thomas.

She knows how important nutrition is in maintaining good health and that it plays a key role in maintaining a stable weight.

You will only reach a stable weight if the calories you consume are the same as the number of calories your body "burns off". She suggests that increasing physical activity and monitoring your food intake by completing a food diary can help start the weight loss journey.

Jevanjot says that your waist size is an important indicator of health risks that you may face. Some health problems are worsened by where your body fat is stored, as well as by your weight. Carrying too much fat around your waist can increase your risk of developing conditions such as heart disease, type 2 diabetes and cancer.

A healthy waist size for all women is 80cm (31.5in) or less. For south Asian men it's 90cm (35in) or less, and for other men it's 94cm (37in) or less.

Although it may seem unfair, research shows that fat around the belly of a South Asian person is more risky than the same amount of fat in a white British person, says Dr Justin Zaman of the South Asian Health Foundation and Consultant Cardiologist at James Paget University Hospital in Norfolk.

Jevanjot also stresses that to maintain a stable weight, does not mean that you need to be on a strict rigid diet and deprive yourself of foods that you enjoy eating. It is about enjoying the food that you eat but having this in the right portions. A balanced diet involves having a variety of foods from different food groups so that you have nutrients from various food sources to be healthy.

She suggests using a shopping list when you do your weekly food shopping. This will help prevent you from buying food that you don't need. Reading food labels will help you to monitor the nutritional value.

The traditional South Asian diet can be healthy. The key is to look at portion sizes and cooking methods to make recipes healthier. For example, we often add potatoes to our curries and then also include chapatti or rice as a staple as well.

Reducing the amount of carbohydrate within the meal can help balance and aid weight loss. Making South Asian meals healthier also means cutting down on fats or oils in cooking, avoiding refrying in the same oil and cutting down on sugar used in puddings and Indian sweets, biscuits and cakes.

She feels that due to work and other commitments many of the South Asians of the second generation's food choices have changed and more convenience and processed foods are being consumed which can be just as unhealthy.

Here are Jevanjot's suggestions for a healthy South Asian diet.

Expert tips for healthier eating

Food or preparation method: Chapatti or roti
The Healthy Way: If wheat flour, change to either medium-brown or wholemeal
Chapattis can also be made from millet flour (Bhajira), maize, cornmeal or gram flour (Basan).

Food or preparation method: Fat added to dough (oil/butter) i.e. Rotali
The Healthy Way: Try not to add any. Keep Chapattis soft by covering with a tea cloth and knead with lukewarm water.

Butter/margarine/ghee – (clarified butter)
Spread onto surface of chapatti
The Healthy Way: Have dry chapatti's, or try low fat spreads or reduce the amount of spreads used.

Food or preparation method: Paronta
Plain Chapatti flour with butter inside, folded and shallow fried on a hot griddle. Can also be made sweet or stuffed savoury stuffed with meat or vegetables
The Healthy Way: Reduce amount in fat in preparation, and try not to add any after cooking.

Food or preparation method: Deep fried small chapattis i.e.
Poori can be spicy or sweet), Bhatura, dhabara, malpula deep fried in ghee (eaten special occasions)
The Healthy Way: Very high in fat. Try not to have often.

Expert tips for healthier eating

Food or preparation method: Pitto steamed (common in Tamil community), Pitta bread, Naan
The Healthy Way: These are healthy options

Food or preparation method: Bread
The Healthy Way: Try to have wholemeal or granary bread

Food or preparation method: Cereal
The Healthy Way: Try to have low sugar and wholegrain variety cereals

Food or preparation method: Rice (white)
The Healthy Way: Best type for diabetes control is white basmati rice as it is low GI. Brown basmati is also available. Try to either boil, steam or microwave.

Food or preparation method: Pilau rice (fried rice)
The Healthy Way: High in fat. Cut down on the oil used.

Food or preparation method: Biriyani, meat or vegetarian
The Healthy Way: High in fat. Try to use low fat cooking methods.

Food or preparation method: Rice flakes (pava) or Manara
The Healthy Way: These are a low fat alternative.

Expert tips for healthier eating

Food or preparation method: Potato
The Healthy Way: Cook with skins on when added to curry. Try to use new potatoes.

Food or preparation method: Meat/chicken, curried, kebab or tandoori
The Healthy Way: Try to cut all visible fat before cooking. Use low fat cooking methods. Skim fat from surface when dish is made. If eaten daily try to reduce frequency and substitute some days with lentils/vegetable curry.

Food or preparation method: Fish white or oily, may be deep fried (masala fish), curried or steamed
The Healthy Way: Try not to fry (masala fish), bake in oven with foil on top. Use yoghurt and tandoori paste as marinade. Try to include oily fish 1-2 times a week.

Food or preparation method: Eggs
The Healthy Way: Have boiled, poached, scrambled. Cut down on oil when cooking omelette or fried egg.

Food or preparation method: Pulses and Dhalls (60 different varieties whole or split) e.g. chickpeas (channa) kidney beans
The Healthy Way: Dhalls can be boiled mashed, dry roasted or fried. Dhall can be ground into flour and used as thickening agent to make pancakes. When cooking dhall cut down on oil used (1-2 tablespoons of oil). Try low fat cooking methods. Avoid adding any butter at the table before

Expert tips for healthier eating

eating. If vegetarian try to have dhall every day for iron. To help absorption of vitamin C – have pure fruit juice or fruit after meal. Try to consume sprouting pulses as they have increased nutritional value.

Food or preparation method: Milk and Dairy products
The Healthy Way: Include 2-3 servings a day

Food or preparation method: Milk used in sweet dishes, mava and khova
The Healthy Way: Do not use gold top Jersey or evaporated or condensed milk. If overweight, advised to have semi-skimmed or skimmed milk. The milk tastes thinner but still full of the goodness.

Food or preparation method:Yoghurt
The Healthy Way: Encourage to buy low fat or make at home with semi-skimmed milk. Do not add fried gramflour balls (boondi). Add cucumber (raita) and tomato instead.

Food or preparation method: Paneer (curd cheese)
The Healthy Way: Try not to fry. Put into low fat curries either scrambled or just cut into cubes. Make paneer with semi-skimmed milk. If having cheese try to have low fat varieties.

Food or preparation method: Fruit and Vegetables have 5 a day
Fruit
The Healthy Way: Encourage to eat all fruit, but for diabetes be cautious of very sweet fruits e.g., mango, grapes etc. Small portions only.

Expert tips for healthier eating

Generally recommend 3 servings per day and spread these out. Where possible, eat with the skins. Try to have dried fruit as a snack or add fruit to breakfast cereals. Try to have tinned fruit in natural juice rather than syrup.

Fruit juice

Try not have sweetened juice drinks. Only small glass of pure juice if taken, as still high in natural sugars. Best to take with food to slow down absorption.

Vegetables

i.e. aubergine, spinach, tomato, okra, peas and cauliflower. Can be made with a sauce, deep fried, stuffed or steamed. Encourage low fat vegetable curry. Try not to overcook or reheat vegetables as this reduces vitamin content, (especially spinach (saag). Encourage salad with meals. Store vegetables in cool dark place and use while fresh

Food or preparation method: Snack foods e.g. biscuits, cakes, pastry

The Healthy Way: Avoid sweet Pakistani rusks. Try to reduce the frequency of biscuits and cakes in general.

Food or preparation method: Bhajis, pakoras, samosas, papad (fried or roasted)

The Healthy Way: Cut down, as these are very high in fat and salt. Best to have fresh fruit. Limit fried foods. If frying, shallow-fry instead of deep-fat frying and remove excess fat using kitchen roll, or bake samosas in the oven. Try tea cakes, toast and crumpets.

Expert tips for healthier eating

Food or preparation method: Chevra (Bombay mix) Nuts (dry roasted or deep fried)
The Healthy Way: Try to have dry roasted nuts i.e. chickpeas or peanuts or popcorn instead of high fat snacks e.g. chevra, gartia, sev or crisps.

Food or preparation method: Dokora, handva (savoury cakes) kama, iddli (steamed)
The Healthy Way: These can be made with less oil and steamed or baked.

Food or preparation method: sugary foods e.g. Indian sweetmeats: (barfi, jelebi and ladoo)
The Healthy Way: High in fat and sugar. Try to avoid Asian sweets – save these only for special occasions. Try to have fruit instead.

Food or preparation method: Puddings e.g. Sevia, Keer, Halva
The Healthy Way: use semi-skimmed milk. Use sweetener for taste or dried fruit, sultanas and raisins. In puddings – try margarine instead of ghee and reduce the quantity. Save for special occasions. If not overweight, can have puddings made with low fat milk and artificial sweetener.

Food or preparation method: Squash/soft drinks/cordial
The Healthy Way: Diet or low-cal, try having occasionally – try sugar-free drinks.

Expert tips for healthier eating

Food or preparation method: Sweet paan
The Healthy Way: Avoid. Have savoury version instead.

Food or preparation method: Sugar, honey, gurr (jaggary), in sweet or savoury foods. Glucose drinks
The Healthy Way: Try to cut down on these, or use artificial sweetener e.g., Canderel, Sweetex.

Food or preparation method: Tea/coffee
The Healthy Way: Check the amount and type of milk used and have low fat milk. Check if sugar, gurr or if honey is added. If necessary use artificial sweetener.

Food or preparation method: Fats e.g. butter ghee, margarine
The Healthy Way: Use pure cooking oil, mono or polyunsaturated, rapeseed or olive oil, sunflower or corn oil instead of ghee or butter. Measure the amount of oil used and try to reduce the quantity used. Aim for half a tablespoon per person in curries. Avoid frying, try to grill, bake, steam or microwave.

Food or preparation method: e.g takeaways, weddings, parties, relatives (weekends); Temple/place of worship.
The Healthy Way: Check type of food eaten and how often involved. Try to be sensible and eat small quantities of high fat and sugary foods.

Food or preparation method: Pickle

The Healthy Way: *High in fat and salt, drain oil before eating. Or try to make pickle with lemon juice or vinegar or have chutneys i.e. tomato, mango or mint*

Reference: from the Multicultural Handbook of Food, Nutrition and Dietetics Paperback – 23 March 2012 by Aruna Thakur

Chapter Ten

Asian culture, how to party, celebrate and stay thin

I am healthy and slim and I enjoy life. This does not mean I

do not go to parties and celebrations, I do and I love them.

I have fun and stay thin. Here is how I do it.

With Indian culture being full of celebrations, parties and family get togethers, it can be hard to control your temptations as there is so much emphasis placed around food. During the summer, the wedding season is in full swing and there are also other celebrations that take place throughout the year such as Vaisakhi, Diwali and Eid. During each of these celebrations there is a lot of food involved and Indian sweets are given as gifts by family and friends.

Also after a wedding it is common for the bride's and groom's family to give Indian sweets to the guests to thank them for attending. One year I attended 15 weddings and we had 15 boxes of Indian sweets given to us! With 15 weddings to go to I had to stop myself from over indulging on all of that food spread out in front of me and stop myself from munching on those 15 boxes of Indian sweets!

During my niece's wedding we were celebrating all week and getting together; with the main ceremonies consisting of a ladies night, a pre-wedding party and then the actual wedding day. You can only guess that there was a lot of calorific fattening food served during the week.

A typical Indian wedding will involve the serving of samosas, onion bhajis, spring rolls, kebabs, fish and chicken served as a starter. By the time you've had one you will want another and another and before you know it you will have lost that sense of control and will have had one too many, enough to make you feel fat and overloaded. It doesn't just end there, as even before you've had time to digest the first course; the second course will be served, which usually consists of naan or chapattis, rice and about 3 curries rich in cream and butter, finished off with a very sugary dessert. The food will taste gorgeous with all the flavours from the spices, but you can only imagine how much weight you will have put on during the three days and how many calories you will have consumed!

You will be shocked to know that there are around 190 calories in two onion bhajis, 289 calories in one samosa, 589 calories in a lamb curry, 260 calories in a vegetable curry, 262 calories in rice, 317 calories in naan, 103 calories in a piece of barfi (Indian sweet) and other sugary deserts such as rasmalai can have up to 250 calories per serving.

Let's say you had two onion bhajis, one samosa, some lamb curry and some vegetable curry, rice, nann and a desert, you would be consuming a shocking 1895 calories in just 2 meals! Consuming this amount of food is ok once every now and again, but if you have a party too many this could be a problem and will not help you with your weight and before you know it you will not be able to get into your Indian outfits.

In my experience and for most of my clients, controlling your temptations with food during these celebrations is a battle of the mind. On one hand you want to eat all of the delicious food spread out in front of you and on the other hand you don't want to consume all of those calories and pile all that weight on.

One client, Kam, that I worked with struggled with pressure during any celebration as saying no to food or restricting herself to small portions was seen as a sign that she does not like the food and this was taken as offence.

My client felt that she had to eat more than she needed to as this kept the family happy and it showed that she enjoyed the food even though she felt awful for it afterwards. Another client, Amita, felt that it was rude to say no to food if someone offers it to you and said that even though you say no to a second helping, the family will pile it on your plate anyway. With these family pressures it can be hard to control your weight if you have lots of celebrations to attend.

During any celebration or festive occasions where there is a lot of food involved it is so important that you learn to take control of your temptations and learn to stop when you are full, even though you enjoy the food so much that you could eat until you are stuffed to the brim. Taking control will help you to keep your weight under control and will ensure that you don't pile anymore on.

My tips

Here are a few things that you can do to help you to manage your weight during a celebration.

1) Eat slowly

In order to manage the pressures of your family and friends forcing you to eat more than you need to, eat your food slowly. This will stop them from adding more food to your plate as it will still look full and give the illusion you have already had seconds. I use this technique all the time when I have any celebration to attend.

My client Kam used this technique and said it has worked brilliantly. Eating slowly will also stop you from feeling too full and will help you to digest the food much more easily.

2)   Do you really need three courses?

Ask yourself, if you need a three course meal? Probably, you rarely have a three course meal at home so why eat that much at a party? You could consider limiting yourself to two small courses to help you to manage the calories and you will probably feel less overloaded.

3)   Admire others

Have a look around at all the other ladies and admire how good they look. Instead of feeling sorry for yourself and thinking that you will never reach your target weight and will always look like a fat pudding in your Indian outfit, create a vision of how amazing you will look once you have lost all that weight you have been carrying around. This will mentally make you aware of eating too much and will help you to control your portion sizes. This technique will also help to motivate you that you will look and feel amazing as you move forward with your weight loss journey.

4)   Use self-hypnosis

When that delicious food is put out in front of you, talk to yourself in your head. Keep on telling yourself "I am in control and food no longer controls me". Keep on telling yourself you only need one piece of food to feel satisfied and fulfilled. Remind yourself that party food is very fattening and that the fat will sit on your body like lard. You will feel great afterwards for being in control and resisting the temptation. This will also give you that sense of control.

5)   Have a dance to burn those calories

Instead of thinking about food throughout the whole wedding and how you will satisfy your stomach, why not get on the dance floor instead. Dancing will divert your attention away from picking at the food and it will also give you a chance to socialise with others. If you don't fancy having a dance, walk around to meet other people. Do anything to stop you from thinking about food.

6) Weight loss hypnotherapist

You may even consider enlisting support from a weight loss hypnotherapist who will help to programme your mind so that you can take back control over food so that it does not dominate and control your whole life. They will help you to achieve a positive mindset and give you that enthusiasm to do something about your weight. A good weight loss hypnotherapist will also teach you self-hypnosis so that you can use this wonderful technique in your own time and when you are put to the test with indulging on too much food.

These are just some simple motivational techniques that can be used by anyone, so next time you go to a party or feel you are losing control try these simple techniques and see how you get on.   And if you need more help then contact me. That's all for now and I wish you well with your weight loss journey.

I want to finish with a role model for any of us. Foja Singh who is over 100 years old.

He talks about his diet in these terms. He says: "I could go on and on, but it's not a new or magic thing, is it? Punjabi people know eating and drinking is important, but I just eat the minimum of what I need: some daal and roti, gobi and chai – I'd probably be dead if I was full all the time."

Want to know more?

Then visit me at Slim and Spicy on Facebook

Or contact me at

http://www.yourweightlosswhippet.co.uk/contact/

and quote the code Manjit 123 to get extra

materials, free offers and special deals.

Slim and Spicy

Printed in Great Britain
by Amazon